FROM

EMBERS

TO A

FLAME

FROM

EMBERS

TO A

FLAME

How God Can
Revitalize
Your Church

HARRY L. REEDER III
WITH DAVID SWAVELY

PUBLISHING
P.O. BOX 817 • PHILLIPSBURG • NEW JERSEY 08865-0817

Page design and typesetting by Lakeside Design Plus

Printed in the United States of America

Library of Congress Cataloging-in-Publication Data
Reeder, Harry L., 1948–
    From embers to a flame : how God can revitalize your church / Harry L. Reeder III, with David Swavely.
       p. cm.
    Includes bibliographical references and index.
    ISBN 0-87552-512-1
    1. Church renewal—Biblical teaching. I. Swavely, David, 1966–.
II. Title.

BS680.C48R44 2004
253—dc22

2004044157

Contents

Acknowledgments

How can I, in such a brief space, thank so many people? Thanks go to P&R Publishing for agreeing that this is a needed book, and to Dave Swavely, who crafted it so well.

I owe thanks to the Briarwood Church membership and leadership, for allowing and supporting this endeavor, and to my administrative assistant, Marie Gathings, for her able and encouraging support. I also want to thank Pinelands Presbyterian Church and Christ Covenant Church, where I had the privilege to serve.

I'd like to thank my sisters, Vickie, Beth, and Amy, along with their husbands. And it is an enormous blessing to be supported by my children Jennifer, Ike, and Abigail, along with my grandchildren, Brianna, C.J., and Mack.

Especially, I want to dedicate this book to my wife, Cindy, the one through whom I came to Christ and with whom I have been able to serve Christ; and to my dad and mom, who wanted to see this project finished but in God's providence both were promoted to heaven this past year.

Finally, I thank all of those faithful pastor-shepherds serving Christ's sacred church in difficult, trying, and challenging situations. I salute and honor you. More than that, the Lord will honor you as you are faithful. I hope this book helps you lead His church to vitality and influence as you *remember, repent, and recover the "first things."*

Introduction

Imagine that you are a recent seminary graduate and have just begun your first pastoral ministry. The church you have been called to serve was at one time among the largest and fastest growing in the region. It had risen to a membership of almost nine hundred, with four major worship services and a vital Sunday school program. It was known for creative and effective ministries, an innovative youth program, an expanding Christian day school, and a significant commitment to world missions.

Now, twenty-five years later, the average Sunday morning attendance is below eighty. The Sunday school has fallen to fewer than twenty adults with no children. The average age of the members is around sixty-nine. At age thirty-three, you are the youngest member of the congregation, with the exception of your wife and children. Sunday evening services have been cancelled, and it is considered a notable victory if five people come to the midweek prayer service. Vandalism occurs daily on the church grounds, and minimal amounts of money are now going to missions and benevolence. The church preschool has supported the church with its meager surplus, yet not one family or faculty member from the school is attending the church.

In your first week at the church, a representative from the denomination calls you and says, "I am on the church-growth committee, and we would like for you to consider a suggestion we have. Now I know that you are new here, and I know that this is your first pastorate in our denomination, but we would like for you to consider talking to your leadership about selling the church building and property, taking the proceeds from the sale, and planting a church somewhere else."

"Excuse me?" you say.

"We would like you to close down. We have been wanting this church to close down for about ten years. So now that you're here, would you consider leading them to close down?" He reminds you that three previous pastors were defrocked, and others have left in abject frustration. In fact, the church has demoralized most of its previous pastors.

Also during your first week, you receive another call, this time from one of those frustrated former pastors.

"We are really glad to have you in the denomination," he says, "but I have to tell you that I have been concerned since I heard that you were coming to this particular church. I used to be the pastor there, and I would rather see you serving somewhere else."

"Why is that?" you ask.

"Well, I believe that church has the mark of Satan upon it."

Not exactly the most encouraging words to hear during your first weeks!

The finance committee informs you that it may be difficult to meet the figure promised to you in your salary, because the church has not met its budget in years.

The local office supply store has flagged your account, and of all the churches in the area yours is the only one that is not allowed credit. You must pay cash only.

You begin a Sunday evening service. The first night your attendance is eleven, and that is the encouraging part. The discouraging part is that five of them belong to your immediate family. One of the others attending is an elder, who asks you to go out to eat after the service, but you tell him that you have to go home after the service to work on some things, because a man is coming the next day to fix your refrigerator.

"Hey, listen, let's go out tonight anyway," he says to you at the front of the church, as you are about to begin the service. "Don't worry about that @#%! refrigerator."

At your first board meeting, you learn that two elders are rotating off, and they will need to be replaced.

"I think so-and-so should be an elder," one of the men says. "I nominate him."

"Is he still a member of this church?" another one asks.

"I don't know," he replies.

"Does he come on Sundays?"

"No, I haven't seen him, but if we make him an elder, maybe he will."

As you get to know the elders better, you realize that some probably do not know the Lord. And within the first month, you lose two godly men—one moves away and the other dies of leukemia.

This wasn't the picture they painted in seminary, and you are about to quit before you get started.

What I just asked you to imagine is not a hypothetical scenario. It is the true story of my first pastoral ministry, at Pinelands Presbyterian Church in Miami. That body had once, long ago, been aflame with excited members, effective ministries, and regular conversions. But by the time I was called there, only embers remained. I desperately wanted to see God ignite those embers into a fire again, so I searched His Word to find the biblical principles that apply to church revitalization. By God's grace, we put those principles into practice, though with many mistakes. And by God's grace the church came alive.

Within three years, we grew to an average attendance of over four hundred. More than half of those added were by conversion or rededication to Christ. But almost as gratifying as the conversion growth was the fact that only one family from the original congregation was lost to another church in the process of revitalization. Instead of feeling disenfranchised or dismantled, the former members became a vital part of the "new work" of the Lord at Pinelands, rejoicing in what the Lord was doing and having a vested interest in the church's ministry and the new vision for the community we served.

Since then, I have had the privilege of leading another church through the process of revitalization. Christ Covenant Church in Charlotte, North Carolina, grew from thirty-eight members to over three thousand in attendance over the course of seventeen years. The Lord also allowed the church to have a significant impact on its community, as it became "salt and light" in many ways around the Charlotte area. We were involved in launching a number of new congregations in the region, and also had the privilege of supporting and participating in many missions ministries throughout the world and sending many of our members to the mission field.

Not every successful church will grow as big as Christ Covenant, of course, but every successful church will certainly experience the power of the Holy Spirit working in it and through it in many visible ways. And I am convinced that this kind of revitalization, when it is truly of God, will happen only as church leaders wisely apply the biblical principles related to the health of a church. In this book, you will learn those principles, and much of the wisdom, that our Lord can use to take any church from embers to a flame!

C H A P T E R

The Need for Church Revitalization

The people of God need a biblical strategy for church revitalization, because so many of us are or will be part of a body that is in need of it. Consider the following information:

- About 95 percent of all churches in North America average one hundred people or less at worship.[1]
- Over 80 percent of established American churches are either on a plateau or in decline.[2]
- Every year 3,500–4,000 churches die in this country.[3]

As Lyle Schaller writes, "An average of fifty to sixty congregations in American Protestantism choose to dissolve every week compared to perhaps five to ten that are able and willing to redefine their role."[4] And Kirk Hadaway, a church-growth research specialist with the Southern Baptist Convention, writes: "The typical church in almost any American denomination is either on a plateau or declining in membership and participation. Rapid growth is atypical, and among older congregations the pattern is even more pronounced—plateau and decline are the rule; growth is the rare exception."[5]

My denomination, the Presbyterian Church in America, is considered one of the fastest-growing groups in our nation. You can see why when you look at our statistics, which indicate, for example, that twenty-eight new churches were established in the PCA during a recent year. That is more per capita than most other denominations. But if you look further, you will also find that in the same year, twenty-four churches were "dissolved," or closed. So we could only claim a net growth of four churches during that particular year. And if that is the case with one of the fastest growing groups in America, you can imagine the struggles facing many of the others!

I would suggest that it is not inevitable that so many churches find themselves "sick" or "dying." The principles discussed in this book will help leaders and members in those churches to rekindle the flames of godly growth in their bodies. And they will also serve as *preventive* measures for currently healthy churches, to keep them from the decline that will inevitably overtake them unless they experience the continuing grace of renewal. But before we begin learning about the cure, we should first diagnose the disease.

SYMPTOMS OF A SICK CHURCH

What happens when a church is plateaued, stagnant, dying, or declining? Or what problems do you want to *avoid* in order to keep a church from sliding down the path to ineffectiveness and regret? Falling numbers in attendance and finances are often a sign of sickness, of course. But there are other, less obvious symptoms that I have observed in churches that need a ministry of revitalization.

A Focus on Programs

Dying churches tend to be focused on programs. Like a gambler looking for a winning ticket, they search for a program that will "turn their church around." They are pinning their hope for success on the latest organized ministry or prepackaged church-growth plan, and they evaluate the health of the church by the number and impressiveness of such programs. In fact, I wouldn't be surprised if some people read this book expecting to find just that—a new program to implement in their church. But they will be disappointed, because this book is not about a *program* that you can use to turn your church around. Rather, this book contains *principles* that the Lord has designed and will use to bring more life to the body as He chooses to do so in His sovereign plan.

The difference is important, because when a program succeeds, it is likely to be credited to the efficiency of the plan or the cleverness of its author. And when one fails, we tend to run off to find the next program, in the hope that it will work better. But when we experience health and growth through the principles that God has provided in His Word, all glory goes to Him alone. And if those principles don't seem to "work," we know it is not God's fault; so we turn back to the Scriptures to find out what we need to understand and do better. As we will discuss more in the next chapter, we should not be looking for something new as a model for revitalization, but should be learning more about the model that God has already given to us in His Word.

Nostalgia and Tradition

Dying churches are often living in the past. In fact, many times a pastor is not actually called to a church with the hope of moving it forward, as should be the case. Rather, the people are hoping that he will move the church *backward,* to recapture the "glory days." Remembering a church's past is important—we will learn more about that in the next chapter—but there is a big difference between remembering the past and living in it.

A few years ago I was asked to visit a church in Louisiana, to give the leaders some counsel about their struggling ministry. At a break in our meeting, one of the deacons walked me down a hallway lined with portraits of all the former pastors. There were quite a few along this "hall of fame," because the church had been in existence since the 1700s. The deacon made comments about many of the men as we walked along, but when we came to a particular man, he stopped in his tracks and stood there in reverent silence. And when he did speak, he did so in hushed tones. The pastor in the picture had come to the church in the mid-twentieth century and had remained there for twenty-five years. It soon became clear to me that this spot in the hall represented the "glory days" of the church, when it was led by *the* pastor. I half expected to see candles on each side of his picture, with an eternal flame burning underneath!

As I talked with the leaders at that church, I realized that everything that happened now was being judged by what happened back then. So I eventually asked them, "If everything was so great back then, why are y'all in the shape you're in now?" I encouraged them to follow the principle in Philippians 3:13, where Paul says he was "forgetting what lies behind and reaching forward to what lies ahead." The past is important and should be celebrated, as we will discuss more in the next chapter. But we need to realize that the pleasant river of nostalgia can swell into a sweeping current that takes the church backward and downward to destruction.

An overemphasis on tradition is another way that the past can haunt a church. At Pinelands Church, for instance, I found a group of not eighty people trying to uphold traditions that were begun when the church was nine hundred strong. You could shoot a cannon filled with grapeshot from front to back and not hit a single person during the morning worship service. Yet some wanted to go to four services on Sunday morning. Why? Because four services were symbolic of the glory days! The logic? Four services would recapture those days. I tried patiently to explain that it wasn't four services that brought the people. It was growth that necessitated the four services.

Personality Dependence

Dying churches tend to rely on certain personality types, whether or not they have such people in the church. If they have a strong leader, they may look to him (or her) to do all the work or make all the decisions. If they are looking for a pastor, on the other hand, they may think that there is only one type of person who can lead them into growth. I remember talking to one pulpit committee that told me, "We could solve all our problems if you could find us a good preacher who has a high D personality." By this they meant an extroverted man who is a "real aggressive leader." But they were under the misconception that God uses only one type of personality in His work of church leadership.

11

I asked them if they had ever met Frank Barker, who is now the pastor emeritus of Briarwood Presbyterian Church in Birmingham, Alabama, where I am presently serving as senior pastor. Frank was the founding pastor and led the church for forty years, during which time it was very successful by any standard. But he is hardly an extrovert or a "high D" personality. Two stories illustrate that fact. First, a man I know once sat for a while in the church library talking to a man that he guessed was the church sexton, only to find out that it was Frank Barker. And one of his staff members once decided to test a little theory when he accompanied Frank on a two-hour drive to Atlanta. He decided he would not say anything at all, but simply wait to see how long it would take Frank to initiate a conversation. Two hours later, Frank finally said, "Is this the city limits?" Yet this quiet, unassuming man led a very successful church for many years.

D. James Kennedy is another example of an effective church leader who is definitely not an extrovert. And there are many others. So be careful not to fall into the trap of thinking that God can only work through certain personality types. He has granted to the church a wide variety of gifts, and He has planned to use a wide variety of people in the building of His kingdom (cf. 1 Cor. 12:4–6).

A Maintenance Mentality

Remember the old "Looney Toons" cartoons where Wile E. Coyote would chase Road Runner off a cliff and then realize he was dangling in midair above certain death? Wile E. would grab the edge of the cliff and hang on until his fingers eventually slipped and he became a brown pancake on the canyon floor. That is the way a lot of churches look at ministry today. "Let's just hold on," they are thinking. "Hopefully we can replace the number of people we lost last year," they say, or "We will be lucky if we can meet our budget." They actually do have a "vision" for ministry, but the vision is "hang on and hold on." It is a maintenance mentality, where they are merely polishing a *monument*, rather than building a *movement* of God's grace. They are on a life-support system, rather than on a life-saving mission. And their only hopes and dreams are to keep the doors open, rather than to bring a harvest of souls through those doors.

Excuses and a "Victim" Mind-set

Another attitude that seems to pervade sick and dying churches is one that says, "It will never work here, because . . ." The leaders and members already have a well-rehearsed list of reasons why a new ministry idea will not be effective. Two classics are "We've tried that before" and "It will cost too much," but others might be "The neighborhood has changed," "Our building is in the wrong place," or "This is a tough, unchurched community." The church has become like a sports team that has lost every game for ten years and already has a list of excuses for the defeats it expects in the upcoming season.

The assumption underlying those excuses is that the church is a *victim* of some outside factor, which keeps it from being greatly used of God. Whether it is a lack of money, a tough location, or whatever, there is a subtle but dangerous mentality that the church is doomed to mediocrity or failure because of its circumstances. These churches have no real hope because they are allowing themselves to be dominated by negative circumstances—a problem that the Bible says we must work hard to avoid (cf. James 1:2–4). In fact, the Scripture teaches us that even our *weaknesses* provide an opportunity for God to work in and through us. Consider what the apostle Paul says in 2 Corinthians 12:8–10:

> Concerning this I entreated the Lord three times that it might depart from me. And He has said to me, "My grace is sufficient for you, for power is perfected in weakness." Most gladly, therefore, I will rather boast about my weaknesses, that the power of Christ may dwell in me. Therefore I am well content with weaknesses, with insults, with distresses, with persecutions, with difficulties, for Christ's sake; for when I am weak, then I am strong.

The believers in Uganda, Africa, illustrate this point well. I have been privileged to minister the gospel during six trips to that country, but I will never forget my first one. It was in the mid-1980s, not long after Idi Amin's war for power and reign of terror had left the nation and its people in unspeakable misery. Among the casualties of that era were many thousands of believers in Christ who were tortured and killed for their faith. While I was there on that first trip, in fact, the new regime uncovered the skeletons of five hundred Christians that had been used as filler and paved over to make a road. Inflation in the economy of Uganda at that time was between 600 and 800 percent, and the people lived under martial law with the constant fear of a new war or the rise of a new dictator who might rape their land.

But there was (and still is, in fact) a great movement of God taking place in and through the churches of Uganda. I remember being asked to preach one day in a bombed-out cathedral, then being asked to preach again after I was finished. And then I was asked to preach again! I said to them, "You want me to preach more? I've already done it twice." And through the interpreter they answered, "Yes, please, we have walked a long way today." I had to flip through my Bible frantically to find something to teach them, because they were so eager to hear the Word of God! And they were reaching out to their friends, also—even during my brief visits, I saw hundreds of people come to Christ.

So even in the midst of great persecution and difficulty, the churches in Uganda were thriving. They did not view themselves as hopeless victims, or use their circumstances as an excuse for defeat. In the same way, many churches in our land need to realize that God is able to bring them new life, no matter how dim their prospects may seem at the present.

Making excuses is so easy and can become such a habit, that we can fall into self-deception and lose touch with reality. I once talked with the leaders of a church who wanted to sell their building and move to another area because, they said, "We just can't minister here anymore." Their reason was that the community had changed over the years. "We used to be able to reach the community because it was people like us, but now it is all Hispanic." I asked them how they knew that, and they told me that a Spanish-speaking church was renting their building on Sunday afternoons, and it had a growing attendance of over four hundred people. The church that owned the building, on the other hand, had only about forty people attending on Sunday morning.

We checked the census records, however, and found out that the community around the church was actually 88 percent Anglo, and less than 12 percent Hispanic! So I told the church, "I have some good news and some bad news for you. The good news is that 88 percent of the people around you speak the same language you do, so you don't have to move. The bad news is that the church renting from you is reaching the other 12 percent and filling the building every Sunday afternoon." I suggested to them that they should be less concerned about moving at this point, and more concerned with what they might be doing wrong, and what they could do right to reach people with the gospel. And I hoped that their sense of responsibility to do so would be greater now that their excuse had been removed.

A Bad Reputation in the Community

Another symptom of a dying church is its perception by others around it. The longer a church follows a pattern of decline, the worse its public image and reputation become. The community at large and the neighboring churches form opinions as to the church's condition. The people who do the most damage in this regard are often the ones who have left the church and gone elsewhere. They find it difficult not to share their "inside" information and "horror stories" about the decline of the church, the lack of resources in the congregation, or how they were mistreated by people in the body. In fact, as a pastor, I have often discovered people who will not listen to a word I say because of the damaging reports they have heard about the church from former members. And, as the years go on, the list of evil rumors becomes longer, and the task of revitalization grows harder.

Sometimes the symptoms of decline can appear *outside* your church before they are even noticed inside. Leaders and members in a church may think that everything is proceeding wonderfully, but the real tale may be told in the world around it, and even in other churches. So I've suggested that pastors and other leaders in a church should regularly ask questions about their congregation when they talk to people on the outside. Two good ones are, What have you heard about our church? and How do you think the community perceives us? When standing in line at the grocery store, ask the person next to you, "Have you ever heard of [your church's name]? What do you make of it? Would you go there?" Then listen carefully. It takes courage, but it can be revealing. Remember that reputation is not what we write on our church bulletins, but what people actually think of us!

Distraction from the Gospel

This final symptom of sickness in a church is actually the worst one of all. Churches that have grown ineffective in reaching the world around them have often done so because they have lost sight of the *centrality* of God's grace. Something else has become more important than living according to the gospel and sharing it with people who need to be saved. Perhaps the priority has fallen on certain doctrinal distinctives, on the physical condition of their buildings, or on a particular method of education. Whatever the emphasis may be, it will be counterproductive to God's work if it is allowed to usurp the rightful place of the gospel as the center of all we do as the people of God.

We will discuss the priority of the gospel much more fully in chapter 3. But if your church has slipped in this regard, or is manifesting any of the other symptoms of decline that I have mentioned, it is in need of revitalization. And if your church has not yet been afflicted with these problems, praise God! But realize that it could succumb to them at any time if the principles we will learn are not practiced for the glory of God.

THE PRIVILEGES OF CHURCH REVITALIZATION

Church revitalization is important because so many churches are dead and dying, and because all healthy churches run the risk of becoming diseased and developing the symptoms of decline that we have discussed. But I want to suggest that there are also a number of *positive* reasons why we should pray and work for church revitalization today. Hopefully, these will encourage those who are in this ministry already, and they may also motivate others to enter it, as the Lord leads them.

The Heart of the Shepherd

If a particular church is dying, the conventional wisdom in some circles is that it should be closed down and perhaps "restarted" somewhere else. There is certainly a time and place for that approach, but I would suggest that in most cases a ministry of church revitalization is closer to the heart of our Lord. He is, after all, the Great Shepherd:

> What do you think? If any man has a hundred sheep, and one of them has gone astray, does he not leave the ninety-nine on the mountains and go and search for the one that is straying? And if it turns out that he finds it, truly I say to you, he rejoices over it more than over the ninety-nine which have not gone astray. Thus it is not the will of your Father who is in heaven that one of these little ones perish. (Matt. 18:12–14)

Those words of our Lord Jesus were directed primarily at individuals (cf. vv. 15–20), but they have an application to churches as well. Look, for instance, at how our Savior pleads with the troubled churches in Revelation 2–3. Yes, there comes a time when the lampstand has to be removed, or when "Ichabod" must be written on the door of the church, but before that, the Lord exhorts the leaders and the congregation to repent and preach and pray for revival (cf. Rev. 3:18–20). So I

think that when a pastor, a supporting church, or a denomination comes alongside a church in need of revitalization, they
are reflecting the heart of God. And when they "dissolve" one
too soon, when there is still hope for change and growth, they
may be grieving the One who leaves the ninety-nine to seek
the stray.

The Heart of the Apostle

In Acts 13, Paul and Barnabas were sent out from the
church at Antioch on what has become known as Paul's First
Missionary Journey. They traveled throughout Asia Minor
with a clear philosophy of ministry:

- gospel evangelism and discipleship,
- gospel church planting,
- gospel deeds of love, mercy, and justice,
- gospel leaders developed and deployed.

In Acts 15, Paul was ready for another round, so he set
off on the Second Missionary Journey. It is interesting to note
that the apostle did not simply say, "Let's go find new places
to spread the gospel." Rather, he said, "Let us return and visit
the brethren in every city in which we proclaimed the word of
the Lord, and *see how they are*" (Acts 15:36). The apostle Paul
renewed his commitment to all the elements of the philosophy of ministry mentioned above, and now he added to them
a fifth objective:

- gospel church revitalization.

Acts 15:41 says that "he was traveling through Syria and Cili-
cia, *strengthening the churches.*" And when he began his Third

Missionary Journey, Acts 18:23 says, "he departed and passed successively through the Galatian region and Phrygia, *strengthening all the disciples.*" If you look at a map of Paul's third trip, in the back of your Bible, you will see that it follows the path of the second trip almost exactly.

So the Great Commission work of the apostle Paul was not just a ministry to unreached places and people, but also a ministry of revitalization. We know that some of these churches were struggling with great difficulties even during Paul's lifetime (just look at his letters to the Galatians and the Corinthians!). Therefore, a major part of Paul's ministry was devoted to bringing declining churches from embers to a flame!

This should be a great encouragement to pastors and others who find themselves in a ministry that needs a lot of help. If some of the churches started by the great apostle were in need of revitalization within a few years, why should we be surprised when this happens today? If Paul's churches suffered from decline, we should not be ashamed or reluctant to admit that ours are hurting, too. And when we have the privilege of working with such a church, we should be excited about being involved in this truly apostolic ministry!

Church Planting or Church Revitalization?

The ministry of starting new churches is a rewarding one, but I would suggest that the ministry of revitalizing existing churches is sometimes even more rewarding. Many would say that church planting is easier to do, especially for young pastors, but I do not think that is necessarily true, for several reasons.

First, consider the people you will be working with. Don McNair's book *The Birth, Care, and Feeding of the Local Church* contains the fruit of his extensive study of, and experience in, church planting.[6] McNair suggests that when a pastor starts a church, it is likely that after three years, 90 percent of the people who attended at the beginning will no longer be there. Or the pastor himself will be gone. I realize that there are many exceptions to this rule, but in my experience I would have to agree that it is indeed the rule. Many of the people who come to a new church *do* end up leaving before too long, perhaps because they couldn't get along anywhere else, and they brought the same problems along with them. Or perhaps they were drawn to the new church in the hope that it would become what they wanted a church to be, and they grew disappointed when it did not develop in the direction they expected it to go.

Most church plants do not attract many people who are mature believers with a missionary zeal, eager to sacrifice themselves to advance the kingdom of God. On the contrary, those who are zealous tend to be zealous about other matters. For instance, they think they know "what a church should be," and the leaders back at their former church stood in the way, so they want to hook up with this smaller group of people so they can have more control over what happens. Or maybe they are just upset with what was happening at another church, and they decide to "try this one out." Or maybe they simply like the idea that it is "something new," and when it is not so new anymore, they lose interest. All this adds up to the fact that in church planting, a typical result will be that about 10 percent of the initial group will remain, but the other 90 percent will eventually end up moving on to another church.

When a pastor receives a call to a church in need of revitalization, however, he inherits a group of people who have stayed with that church through thick and thin. Their weaknesses have probably contributed to its decline, and they may be clinging to dead tradition, but at least they are not "consumers" who will move away for no good reason. They probably also do not all have different ideas about what the church should be, as is often the case in church planting. The people who have stayed with a church during its decline are committed to that ministry in that location. And although people like that will certainly present many challenges of their own, I believe that they can be renewed in their faith and greatly used by God through the principles discussed in this book.

Church revitalization, in many cases, also has the advantage of existing resources. You don't have to worry about buying a property—you just have to worry about reaching the people around it. You don't have to build a building—you just have to fill up the one you already have. In church planting, on the other hand, the leaders can be heavily distracted for years by the hard work and headaches of obtaining such resources. When Steve Brown is asked what a pastor should do when the church starts a building project, he usually says, "Resign!" And my guess is that he's only half kidding. Nothing can chew up and spit out pastors faster than a building project!

So not only does the ministry of church revitalization reflect the heart of God and of Paul, but when it is carried out according to the Word of God, it is also a practical and effective way to meet the current needs of the body of Christ in our land. And I believe this type of ministry could become a catalyst for the large-scale revival we desperately need in America.

The Global Opportunity
The priority and privilege of church revitalization extends far beyond our borders, however, to many other places around the world.

For example, there is a denomination in Egypt called the Evangelical Presbyterian Church, which was planted during the nineteenth century, as I understand, by Scots-Irish Presbyterians. Today, as I understand it, there are about 650 licensed and approved Evangelical Presbyterian churches in Egypt, many with buildings that they own. The last statistics that I saw, however, indicated that only 250 of them have pastors. Only a few of them are growing. So here is a tremendous opportunity to have a major impact on an entire country and an entire culture through church revitalization! We do not have to "sneak in" any Bibles, and we do not have to come in under cover. The Egyptian government allows these churches to function.

Can you imagine what would happen if 650 churches came alive in Egypt? That would be church revitalization not only on a local scale, but also on a national and even *historical* scale! I say that because long ago this Muslim country was actually one of the centers of Christianity. The city of Alexandria, at the mouth of the Nile River, was the location of the greatest theological library in the ancient world. Muslim armies overran Christian North Africa many years ago, but our Lord is able to win back those nations for Himself with the weapons of the Spirit and the power of the gospel. Perhaps He will do it through the revitalization of the many churches that already exist there.

I and some other pastors have been holding conferences on church revitalization here in America since 1992, and in recent years we have seen a wave of interest in this ministry from people in other lands. We now have opportunities to conduct Embers to a Flame conferences in Australia, New Zealand, Korea, Japan, Uganda, South Africa, Scotland, Ireland, England, Romania, and France. And the list is growing. We find ourselves in a time similar to that of Paul's Second Missionary Journey. Gospel work has spread throughout the world, and now it is time not only to continue planting churches through evangelism and discipleship, but also to engage in gospel church revitalization. May God help us to make use of this tremendous opportunity!

So God is working to plant churches in America and overseas, but He is also doing great things through the ministry of church revitalization. I am convinced that the best is yet to come, and that this type of ministry will become an increasingly important part of any strategy for home and foreign missions. If God blesses you with the privilege of playing a part in the revitalization of a church, He can then give you the opportunity, which I have enjoyed, of helping others along the same path, throughout our nation and the world.

For me, it all began when I arrived at that dying church I described in the introduction. After a few weeks there, I began to wonder whether the "experts" were right—that the church should be closed down and moved to greener pastures. I had an appreciation for the zeal of the church-growth authors and their literature, but intuitively I wasn't convinced. I came to believe that this situation was a test for me, like the one Abraham faced when he was told to offer up his son Isaac. Would I continue in obedience to the call of God, despite the conflicts outside and the confusion within? The Bible says that Abraham "considered that God is able to raise men even from the dead" (Heb. 11:19), and I likewise believed that He is able to heal and renew a dying church. So I settled in and searched the Scriptures for anything I could find that related to church revitalization.

And I found more than I had ever dreamed. In fact, I found a specific *case study* of a church that had once been great, but found itself declining and heading for destruction! It seemed that God had put this in the Bible just to help me—and anyone else who wants to see a church renewed by His grace. That divine plan for revitalization is the subject of the next chapter.

QUESTIONS

1. Discuss each of the "symptoms of a sick church," and consider whether they apply to your church. Why or why not?

2. In what ways could you address each of these problems in your body?

3. What are some of the privileges of being involved in a church that needs revitalization? How does this encourage you in your personal ministry?

CHAPTER 2

The Biblical Paradigm for Revitalization

Many church leaders today have embraced a model for ministry that seems to come from Wall Street or Hollywood Boulevard more than from the Bible. They believe that churches grow primarily through the application of successful business principles. Others take an approach that is reminiscent of Hollywood—entertaining people so that they will "have a good time" and want to come back. And the philosophy of some seems to have been borrowed from the psychiatrist's couch, of all places. Their emphasis is on providing support and solutions for our deepest emotional and psychological needs, rather than on the spiritual worship of Jesus Christ. Indeed, most churches today seem to have adopted either the Wall Street/corporate model, the Hollywood/entertainment model, or the psychiatrist/therapeutic model.

Helpful insights can be gained from each of these modern models, but none of them captures a *biblical* approach to church revitalization. When I began to study this topic in the Scriptures, in fact, I did not find a business model, an entertainment model, or a therapeutic model. I found that the Bible uses other images to describe the church, which are more appropriate and informative—images such as family, army, and body. I also found that it contains leadership principles for church revitalization, some of which do not fit very well with those popular models. And I found that there is a practical and helpful *example* of church revitalization that God has provided for us in the Word.

A BIBLICAL "CASE STUDY"

At one time during the first century, the church at Ephesus was one of the greatest in the world. It was one of the four influential "epicenter" churches, along with the ones at Jerusalem, Antioch, and Rome. The apostle Paul had founded it (with the help of such luminaries as Silas, Aquila, and Priscilla), and he stayed there for three years, longer than at any other church. The great preacher Apollos was discipled in the church at Ephesus, and as many as thirteen other churches were started in the surrounding regions as a result of its ministry.

One circumstance, recorded in Acts 19:23–41, reveals how effective those young believers were in influencing the culture around them. False religion, especially the worship of the Greek goddess Artemis, had been big business in Ephesus. Shrines, statues, and other paraphernalia were some of the city's primary commodities. But as the church grew, so many people were being saved from false religion that the idol industry went into recession. The impact of the church was so significant, in fact, that the local craftsmen became afraid that they might be out of a job before too long. They even incited a riot in a desperate attempt to drum up support for pagan worship in their town. A similar situation had developed earlier in Thessalonica, where the unbelievers in the community were saying about the apostles, "These men who have upset the world have come here also" (Acts 17:6). The impact of the believers at Ephesus could be described in the same way—they were "turning the world upside down," as the old translation goes.

So Ephesus was a great church in its early days, making a difference for Christ in its community and in the world. But Paul knew that it could not rest on its laurels. When he said good-bye to the elders, he warned them of the need to stand strong in the face of difficulties to come:

> Be on guard for yourselves and for all the flock, among which the Holy Spirit has made you overseers, to shepherd the church of God which He purchased with His own blood. I know that after my departure savage wolves will come in among you, not sparing the flock; and from among your own selves men will arise, speaking perverse things, to draw away the disciples after them. Therefore be on the alert. (Acts 20:28–31)

Sure enough, false teachers and ego-driven leaders did begin to afflict the church after he left, and this once great church began to decline. The sad process of going from flames to embers had begun by the time the apostle wrote his first letter to Timothy. In that letter he said to Timothy, "Remain on at Ephesus, in order that you may instruct certain men not to teach strange doctrines" (1 Tim. 1:3). Because of its occasion and purpose, in fact, the whole book of 1 Timothy serves as a manual for church revitalization, and all the principles we will be discussing can be found on its pages.[1]

But despite all this instruction from Paul, and the best efforts of Timothy, the church at Ephesus eventually did reach another low point of decline. In the last book of the New Testament, Jesus Himself warned that the church was about to be judged by God, if it did not turn around (Rev. 2:1–5):

> To the angel of the church in Ephesus write:
> The One who holds the seven stars in His right hand, the One who walks among the seven golden lampstands, says this: "I know your deeds and your toil and perseverance, and that you cannot endure evil men, and you put to the test those who call themselves apostles, and they are not, and you found them to be false; and you have perseverance and have endured for My name's sake, and have not grown weary. But I have this against you, that you have left your first love. Remember therefore from where you have fallen, and repent and do the deeds you did at first; or else I am coming to you, and will remove your lampstand out of its place—unless you repent."

Apparently Timothy's ministry of revitalization did have some positive effects, especially in the area of doctrine, because the Ephesians were commended for their discernment regarding false teachers (see v. 6). But they had left their first love and had fallen into a dead orthodoxy, to the point that the Lord threatened to come and remove their "lampstand." This fearful eventuality is described well by the Puritan Matthew Henry, in his commentary on Revelation:

> If the presence of Christ's grace and Spirit be slighted, we may expect the presence of his displeasure. He will come in a way of judgment, and that suddenly and surprisingly, upon impenitent churches and sinners; he will unchurch them, take away his gospel, his ministers, and his ordinances from them, and what will the churches . . . do when the gospel is removed?[2]

That horrible fate was about to befall these believers if they did not turn things around. So if there ever was a church that went from a flame to embers, or from riches to rags, it was the church at Ephesus. But Jesus did not say that the church was without hope, nor did He say that it should be closed down (though that might happen eventually if things did not change). Instead, He provided for us a paradigm, or basic plan, for the revitalization of the church. He told us that a body of believers can arrest its decline and go from embers back to a flame if its leadership will teach it to simply *remember, repent,* and *recover.*

Remember

The first step on the path to revitalization, according to our Lord Jesus, is to "remember . . . from where you have fallen" (Rev. 2:5). We should not live in the past, dominated by nostalgia, as we discussed in chapter 1—but that doesn't mean the past is unimportant. On the contrary, the Scriptures indicate that God wants us to remember the many wonderful things He has done for us and through us. The Psalms, for instance, are filled with recitations of the great works of God from the past. And Joshua 4:20–24 provides an example of the rather

31

curious practice of "piling up stones," which was common in the Old Testament:

> And those twelve stones which they had taken from the Jordan, Joshua set up at Gilgal. And he said to the sons of Israel, "When your children ask their fathers in time to come, saying, 'What are these stones?' then you shall inform your children, saying, 'Israel crossed this Jordan on dry ground.' For the LORD your God dried up the waters of the Jordan before you until you had crossed, just as the LORD your God had done to the Red Sea, which He dried up before us until we had crossed; that all the peoples of the earth may know that the hand of the LORD is mighty, so that you may fear the LORD your God forever."

When I visited Israel for the first time years ago, I expected to see piles of stones sitting around everywhere, because there are so many stories like that in the Old Testament! But notice why the people of God erected such monuments—so that they, their children, and even the world would see the stones and *remember* what God had done. This is crucial because the challenges of today are best met when we look to the Lord and are encouraged by the fact that He has always won the victory. The God who won the victory in the past will win the victory in the present because He is the same yesterday, today, and forever. So the people of God today need to be connected to the past—to the history of their own local church, and also to the history of the church throughout the ages.

The History of the Local Church

A new pastor who comes to an established church needs to realize that the history of that church does not start with him. God has been at work in that body in the past, no matter how troubled it may seem to be now. And the people today, including the present leaders, can gain hope and courage from the good things that God did long before they arrived. As I said before, I'm not suggesting an attempt to return to "the glory days" of the church, and I am certainly not advocating the perpetuation of the *status quo* because "we've always done it that way." You need to move on, but as you do, you should work hard to make a connection to the history of the church.

I have a friend who was called to pastor a church where two famous and successful men had preceded him. Inevitably, someone said to him, "You sure have some big shoes to fill." And my friend replied, "I brought my own shoes, thank you." That is a good illustration of how to avoid the danger of being trapped in the past or dominated by the past. We need to walk in our own shoes, but we also need to be careful not to disrespect or dishonor the ones who have walked before us.

New pastors often make two mistakes when they are intimidated or insecure because of the success of the previous pastor. One is that they attempt to demean the former ministry in order to substantiate their own, and the other is that they attempt to duplicate the ministry of the previous pastor. Both approaches must be avoided at all costs. Of course, if the previous ministry was immoral in some way, you should distance yourself from that sin. But you should appreciate and commemorate whatever was good about the former leaders of the church.

It is good to show honor to them where honor is due—especially in the early years of a revitalization ministry. By building a bridge to the past and celebrating those people and events that are worth celebrating, you can motivate the long-time members to return to their first love, and you can also create a greater bond between them and the newer attenders.

Celebrating the church's history also has a way of balancing the misguided zeal of those who might want to change everything about the church—even the good things!

What are some practical ways to celebrate the past in your church? A retiring pastor, for example, should be honored in various ways—a banquet, appreciation gifts, and perhaps a pastor emeritus position in which he can continue to serve the church in the years to come. You could set aside a Sunday each year to remember what God has done in the history of your church—some call this a "Homecoming Sunday" or "Founders Week." The pastor can incorporate stories from the past into his sermons, or ask people who have been around to share testimonies of special milestones in the life of the church. Be careful that you do not twist the history to fit your own preferences or agenda, but find the things that are truly commendable, and wave them like a flag for the cause of the future ministry of the gospel.

The History of the Universal Church

Another way you can "pile up some stones" and connect to the past is by reminding people that they are part of a glorious river of church history that has flowed from the time of Christ until now. All too often, believers tend to think of themselves only as part of the small pond of modern American Christianity, and they end up becoming stagnant, like the water in many such ponds. But the history of the church is much more like the Mississippi than the local fishing hole, and Christians tend to grow more when they get out of the pond and into the river. This is because their minds are broadened by the pastors and teachers of the past (cf. Eph. 4:11), and because their hearts are challenged by the many great heroes who have gone before.

The way that a church worships, for example, can either connect it to the past or effectively sever it from history. We join ourselves with saints through the ages when we recite historic confessions of faith like the ancient Apostles' Creed or the Westminster Catechisms from Puritan England. And there are many great old hymns that God's people have sung for generation after generation—these should not be jettisoned from our worship just because people may be unfamiliar with their musical style or lyrical depth. Nothing good comes easy, and with a little time and work, people can learn to enjoy older music. We don't want to go to the other extreme and imply that no good music has been written since the nineteenth century, of course, but we should maintain some kind of balance between the past and the present. God is the God of today, *and* He is the God of the ages—and those aspects of His nature should be reflected in our worship.[3]

Good worship does not engage in the arrogance of modernity, which disconnects from the past, nor does it participate in the idolatry of traditionalism, which lives in the past. Rather, we should begin with the great classical worship that at one time was contemporary and has now become tried and true, and then build upon it, being ready to absorb that which is excellent in the present. Good worship is offered in spirit and in truth, honors Christ, and facilitates the praise of God's people and the communication of the gospel to the lost. It is connected to the past without living in the past, contextualized in the present without accommodating the present, and setting a pattern to shape the future instead of becoming dated in the future. Thus it becomes an example of our overall philosophy of ministry.

For many years, I have attempted to connect people to the past by portraying historical figures in special first-person sermons. On Reformation Sunday evening, for example, I have often delivered a message "in character," as if I were Martin Luther, John Knox, or some other hero of the faith who had come to visit. On the Sunday near July 4, I have pretended to be a historical figure commenting on the Christianity of George Washington, Abraham Lincoln, or Patrick Henry. Such messages have been received enthusiastically over the years and have raised the congregation's awareness of the work of God in history. You may not want to do exactly what I've done, but you should find some way to instruct your people in this regard. Adding more illustrations from the past into the Sunday sermons, for example, can be a good way to do that.

Finally, one more way that you can move people from the pond into the river is to teach them about the Old Testament. Just as the history of God's people did not begin with our local church, so it did not begin with the New Testament church. God was calling out a people for Himself for thousands of years before Christ, and therefore the history of Israel is our history, too. As 1 Corinthians 10:11 says, "These things happened to them as an example, and they were written for our instruction, upon whom the ends of the ages have come." Our Lord caused the hearts of the disciples on the road to Emmaus to burn within them as "beginning with Moses and with all the prophets, He explained to them the things concerning Himself in all the Scriptures" (Luke 24:27). The Old Testament is not just a collection of stories teaching moral lessons, but a glorious, progressive unfolding of the majesty of Christ the Redeemer. In other words, it is Christ who is the rainbow, it is Christ who is the arch, it is Christ who is the temple, it is Christ who provides the coat of righteousness, it is Christ who is the ladder that has come down. Such preaching inflames the hearts of God's people as they see the covenant of grace being revealed throughout the Scriptures and then blossoming into the glory of the New Testament.

The Scriptures of Israel constitute over two-thirds of the Bible, and the New Testament without the Old Testament would be like a tree without a trunk (see Rom. 11:17–24). To ignore that important part of God's Word is to miss much of what He has revealed.

So a church that is alive and healthy will be a "movement ministry," rather than a "maintenance ministry." Maintenance ministries live in the past and hang on in the present. But a movement ministry will learn intentionally from the past and then live effectively in the present to transform the landscape of the future. In light of this, I encourage you again to do three things:

- Investigate past blessings.
- Contemplate the lessons and principles that the Lord blessed in the past.
- Celebrate them and continue to implement them in ways that fit the gifts and resources that you currently have in your church.

This will place your ministry within the movement of God's grace and glory from the past into the present to change the future. Our God is the same yesterday, today, and forever. What he has done in the past he can do again.

REPENT

As you investigate and contemplate the past, however, you may realize that there are some things in it that are not worth celebrating. In fact, in the history of a declining or dead church, there are almost always some things that were dead wrong—which means that the church is in need of repentance. This is not as depressing as it sounds, because it presents an *opportunity* for God to do a new and exciting work in the church when we humble ourselves, repent, and pray (cf. 2 Chron. 7:14). It may be that God has been withholding His blessing because the body has not repented, and when it does, He will open the floodgates and pour out His grace in unprecedented measure.

To bring about this corporate repentance, however, you will first have to *encourage the confession of sin* by creating an atmosphere of grace. It's not good enough just to say, "We need to repent. Okay, let's all repent." True repentance begins with confession, and people do not feel free to admit their sins until they understand the gospel of God's free forgiveness. Jack Miller explains this in his excellent book *Repentance and 20th Century Man:*

> If conviction of sin is demanded as though this were the goal of things, if human unrighteousness is exposed apart from faith in Christ, then men will be left suspended in a state of penance, and they will return to pre-Reformation misery, with salvation made entirely unstable because it is founded on what man does to recover himself.
>
> Sinners in such a state have no way of knowing whether God loves them and will receive them to his heart. Psychologically and morally, all is left dark and shoreless. When sin is exposed apart from the promises of God, reality for the man outside of the Lord becomes increasingly inverted and twisted. The aching conscience cannot possibly find relief in this way.[4]

In other words, repentance can only be genuine and lasting when the evildoer sees that God's mercy is available to him. Put grace in an unreachable realm and you simply deepen the convicted sinner's despair and opposition to God. But John's Gospel banners forth the absolutely finished character of Jesus' work (John 4:34, 17:4, 19:30). There is enough love, and more, accessible to any sinner who wants it. One drop of Jesus' blood will, as it were, atone for the worst of man's sins. How then can we fail to respond when we are assured that cleansing love flows in *superabundance* from Calvary?[5]

You must also *emphasize personal responsibility* by discouraging excuse-making. Ever since the very first sin, people have been blaming someone or something other than themselves. We are experts at "playing the victim." When Adam was confronted by God after his sin, his response was, "The woman whom Thou gavest to be with me, she gave me from the tree" (Gen. 3:12). Adam was so intent on shifting the blame from himself, that he managed to accuse both God and his wife in one sentence! And of course the woman did the same thing. When questioned by God, Eve said, "The serpent deceived me" (Gen. 3:13).

There are two ways we can respond when we have sinned: we can cover up or we can "fess up." And one of the primary ways that we cover up is by thinking of ourselves, or speaking of ourselves, as the victims of someone else's mistakes. But whether it is "I have a dysfunctional wife," "The devil made me do it," or any other blame-shifting technique, we need to realize that the blessing of God will not fall on us until we stop making those excuses. First Corinthians 10:13 says that God "will not allow you to be tempted beyond what you are able, but with the temptation will provide the way of escape also." Although we may be tempted by the failures of others, we are never forced into sin. The environment or the occasion does not make us sin. It may influence us, it may draw out the spiritual weaknesses in our own personal life, but it does not force us to sin. The choice to disobey God is ours alone, so we have only ourselves to blame. And the same is true of any church that has failed God in the past. Therefore, confession must begin with personal ownership and agreement with God that we are responsible for the sins that we have committed.

To see a church turn around, we must also *expect the fruits of repentance.* John the Baptist told the multitudes, "Bring forth fruits in keeping with your repentance" (Luke 3:8), which means that repentance is not real unless it issues in action. And 2 Corinthians 7:10–11 teaches this same truth:

> For the sorrow that is according to the will of God produces a repentance without regret, leading to salvation; but the sorrow of the world produces death. For behold what earnestness this very thing, this godly sorrow, has produced in you: what vindication of yourselves, what indignation, what fear, what longing, what zeal, what avenging of wrong! In everything you demonstrated yourselves to be innocent in the matter.

The "fruits" of repentance mentioned in these verses can be summarized in three words: restitution, restoration, and reconciliation. Restitution is paying back what is owed, restoration is setting things right again, and reconciliation is the renewing of relationships that have been broken by sin.

That is just a brief explanation of the nature of repentance according to the Bible. To learn more about the principles related to it, you can read Jack Miller's book mentioned above, or *The Peacemaker,* by Ken Sande.[6] But the concepts I have provided above should be enough for you to understand the following discussion about their application to a church in need of revitalization.

Repentance in the Leaders

Many times a renewal in the body must start with a renewal of certain key members, like the pastor himself. Any kind of "sin in the camp" is damaging to the ministry of a church, as the story of Achan in Joshua 7 illustrates, but nothing is worse than when it is located in the leaders. So God's pathway to repentance for the people often starts with the repentance of those who pastor them. If the ones who lead refuse to confess and turn from their own sin, on the one hand, there will be little hope for the congregation. But, on the other hand, what blessing comes to us when we deal with our sin in God's way!

Early in my ministry as a preacher, I was preparing a sermon on 2 Corinthians 7, the passage about repentance that I mentioned above. As I studied it, I became convicted of a sin I had committed two years before in college. I was taking a Greek exam, and was struggling with a particular translation issue, when the student in front of me stood up to go sharpen his pencil. And there was the answer I needed, right in front of me. So I copied it down on my test, handed it in at the end of class, and went on with my life. But now the Lord was bringing it back to my mind, and I knew I was facing another test at that moment—a test of integrity, a test of repentance. Would I live out the principles that I was learning from the text, and preparing to preach to that congregation? Or would I stand before them as a hypocrite?

Thankfully, I left my notes on my desk and drove over to the college, which was nearby, to see the professor who had taught that class. I told him what I had done, half expecting him to say "That's okay" and send me on my way. But he said, "Well, you know the consequences," and then proceeded to search through his records until he found mine from that year. He marked a zero for my exam grade, and then recalculated my grade for the entire course, which ended up going from a B to a D minus. We prayed together, and I went skipping out of that place, feeling as if the weight of the world had fallen from my shoulders. Not only had I repented and been forgiven for my sin, but I was able to make it right. And now I could stand in front of the church with a clean conscience and teach them how to deal with their own sins.

Pastor or church leader, you may not want to confess your sin, or make restitution for it, because you think it will do more harm than good. You may be worried about your reputation and even the effect it might have on others. But you must understand that you are hurting yourself much more by not repenting, and you are also hurting the rest of the church more by covering that sin. On the other hand, confession brings about the wonderful opportunity of forgiveness, and sets the right example for others who need to deal with their own problems. Remember what the wise man said: "He who conceals his transgressions will not prosper, but he who confesses and forsakes them will find compassion" (Prov. 28:13). While the circle of confession need only to be as wide as the circle of sin, we must "set things right," "avenging the wrong."

Repentance in the Church

Sometimes churches are stagnant or declining because there is "sin in the camp" on a broader level. There is a need for corporate confession, because the body as a whole has not followed God's Word faithfully. I found examples of this when I first arrived at Pinelands Church in Miami, the revitalization project I mentioned earlier. I read thirteen years of minutes from the elders' meetings, and discovered numerous ways that the church had failed to practice the Scriptures. Then I sat down with the current elders and went through them. We prayed for forgiveness, then began a process of making it right. We compiled the names and numbers of over four hundred people who had left the church in recent years, and then we spent two whole weeks calling every one of them. My standard speech went something like this:

> Hello, I am Harry Reeder, the new pastor at Pinelands. I was looking back over the records of the membership and noticed that you used to be a member here. We have come to an awareness in our church leadership that we have not been faithful in ministry to the Lord or to the people. So on behalf of the elders I am calling you and asking for your forgiveness. We have so many unpaid bills of ministry responsibility. Would you forgive us please? And if there is anything in particular where we have wounded you personally, would you give us the opportunity to make that right? We would love to do that.

After that part of the conversation, I would ask them to pray for us that we would be effective in serving the Lord from then on. And then I would ask them if they had a church home, and if not, I would invite them back. Out of four hundred calls, only four families came back to the church. But that was fine, because two of them were troubled marriages on the brink of divorce, which God put back together through our ministry to them. And one of the men who returned ended up serving as a deacon a few years down the line. The greatest blessing that came from this process, however, was the freedom of knowing we were forgiven, by God and by many of those people. And what we did also put an end to a lot of the negative talk about our church in the community—it's harder to say bad things about someone who has asked for your forgiveness and prayers. When you ask for forgiveness from people who have left the church during its difficult times, they lose the need to say negative things about it. In fact, in this case, some were saying things like this: "I left Pinelands, but I hear there is a 'new day' and the Lord is blessing. I am excited about that and we are now praying for them."

There may also be specific sins that the church needs to repent of before it can move on to revitalization. Shortly after I began at Pinelands, for example, I went to a nearby office store to get some supplies. At the cash register, I asked if the store had billing accounts for businesses, and then asked the cashier to put it on our bill. She told me that she couldn't do that, however—the church had been flagged as "cash only" because of repeatedly late payments. So I had to ask forgiveness from the management on behalf of the church, and begin to earn their trust again. I also found out that a former pastor had been involved in a sexual scandal and was actually stabbed by his wife in a local mall, which was all over the papers in the area. But the church never carried out biblical church discipline on the man. So we had to confess that sin and make sure that the whole church now understood the way it should have been handled.

Your situation may be very different from those examples. But when a church is in need of revitalization, there are usually past sins that must be dealt with. Perhaps a previous pastor or some elders have been dealt with treacherously. Perhaps some members have not been shepherded and cared for. Perhaps biblical standards have been abandoned for the sake of pragmatism. Whatever has been happening, the leaders need to lead the church in repentance. Don't take it and put it under the floor of the tent, like Achan did. Confess it, turn from it, and do the deeds that are appropriate to repentance. That is what the gospel allows us to do, with its offer of free and full forgiveness. And that is what the gospel calls us to do.

RECOVER

Jesus told the church at Ephesus, "I have this against you, that you have left your first love. Remember therefore from where you have fallen, and repent and *do the deeds you did at first*" (Rev. 2:4–5). The New International Version translates that verse this way: "Repent and do the things you did at first." So our Lord's paradigm for the revitalization of a church includes remembering the past, repenting from mistakes that have been made, and then *recovering* the "first things."

Back to the Basics

The concept of recovery is very helpful in understanding the task of church revitalization, for several reasons. First, it sheds light on one of the problems with most of the modern models for church growth and renewal. Whether it is the business model, the entertainment model, or the healing model, they all have one thing in common: they are *new* strategies for growing the church in the modern world. But Jesus doesn't say that we should *reengineer* the church; He says that we should *reestablish* it. He calls for a return to the "first things" that made the ministry great before, not for a whole new approach to "doing church."

I once heard a story about the legendary football coach Vince Lombardi, when his Green Bay Packers had lost a game to the New York Giants by a wide margin. The players came to practice the next day hanging their heads, expecting to be dressed down by their coach in royal fashion. As they sat before him waiting for his speech, he paced back and forth in silent agitation. But then he surprised them by simply picking up a football and holding it in front of them. "Gentlemen," he said deliberately, "this is a football." Lombardi then proceeded to expound the most basic features of the sport, as if they were first graders who had never heard of it before.

The coach's point was that they had not lost because of a lack of complexity in their game plan, nor because the other team had come up with some subtle strategy. They lost because they did not block well and tackle well and practice the other basics of football. And to win the next week, they needed to get back to the basics and do them right. This is similar to what our Lord says to a church that has been declining, and it is encouraging to know that we don't need to be rocket scientists (or marketing experts, entertainers, etc.) to see a church go from embers to a flame. We just need to get back to the "first things," which we will be discussing throughout the rest of this book, and do them well.

Health and Growth

The term *recovery* is used in the medical field, and that makes it appropriate for church revitalization, because our goal should be to have a *healthy* church. So many pastors and church leaders today are striving for church growth, but that is putting the cart before the horse. The objective should not be church growth, but church health, because growth must proceed from health.

When my children were growing up, my wife and I did not stand them next to the height marks on the wall and say, "Now by next year you must be taller than this mark. We will be very disappointed if you are not." We did not make growth our goal for them, but we focused on feeding them and caring for them. And we knew that if they were healthy, they would grow.

The church works the same way. If a body is healthy, it will grow. And although growth in the church will usually include more people coming, that is not always the case.[7] So we should focus on the health of the church and let God take care of the growth. If you do it the other way around, you may end up with an unhealthy church that has a lot of people—one that may look successful, but is not really pleasing to God.

The size of a church body is not necessarily an indication of its health—just as it is with human bodies. I have known some people with big bodies who were healthy, and others who were not. I have known people with small bodies who were healthy, and some who were not. We have all seen how obesity destroys a body and how a refusal to eat can emaciate a body. But if a body is healthy, it will then be proportionately the right size. Even so, whether a church is healthy depends not on its size, but on what is happening inside it. This is an important perspective to remember today, when many are criticizing big evangelical churches for being "a mile wide and an inch deep." That is truly a danger, but I would suggest that the other extreme is also a problem. In reaction to the superficiality of the day, some churches are becoming "a mile deep and an inch wide." They are like small, exclusive clubs where the "initiated" are highly initiated, but they are also highly ineffective at reaching the lost for Christ.

So our focus should be primarily on the health, or *vitality*, of the church. That is why I like the term *revitalization*, even though it is a mouthful. It places the emphasis where it belongs. You do not need a marketing plan to grow the church; you need a biblical fitness plan to promote its health. And you should be preoccupied, not with *programs* designed to produce numbers, nickels, and noise, but with biblical *principles* by which the Holy Spirit can bring health and vitality to the body of Christ.

Scaffold or Foundation?

Finally, the idea of recovery calls to mind the importance of the existing congregation in a ministry of church revitalization. One of the foremost responsibilities of a leader in such a situation is to help members recover the "first things" that they have lost. And their participation in the new ministry will be an important factor in the future of the church.

I have encountered two very different perspectives on the congregation among the pastors attempting revitalization projects. Some view their inherited members as a "scaffold" upon which they must temporarily stand while they build a new work. The older members are seen as an expendable entity. If they become part of the new work, fine. But those who do not fit into the new work are, like scaffolds, dismantled and cast aside.

I consider this "scaffold" perspective a callous misuse of Christ's church. It operates on the pragmatic principle that the end justifies the means. But the fact is that the means *determine* the ultimate end, and such an approach will not end up being pleasing to God or good for the church. This is because the older members need pastoral care. They have been wounded and discouraged as they have watched their church weaken and come near to dying. And their spiritual needs have not always been met as the church has limped along. What they need least of all now is a pastor who manipulates them for some "higher ends" he has in mind. Their souls are also precious in God's sight, and if you are their shepherd, then they are your first responsibility. In fact, the pastor's relationship with the existing congregation, however weak or small it may be, sets the tone and creates the environment for everything else he hopes will happen. Yes, many of the more "spiritual" people have left the church, but those who have stayed for institutional reasons should not be dishonored, but should be treated with respect.

So the perspective I recommend is one in which the inherited congregation is viewed as a "foundation" for the potential congregation. These people are not leftovers, but a flock of God that has been suffering and is in need of the healing touch of a shepherd. The integrity of the pastor in dealing lovingly with those whom the Lord has given him will be the determining factor for both the quality and the quantity of the future congregation that he hopes will emerge.

The first part of my ministry of revitalization at Pinelands was not spent in advertising, neighborhood canvassing, or new program implementation. I began by first visiting the families of the existing congregation, accompanied by an elder. For many it was the first time in years a pastor or elder had been in their homes on a ministerial visit. In fact, one family told me it was the first time in twenty-two years that a pastor had been in their home. Is it any wonder that the church was dying?

PUTTING "FIRST THINGS" FIRST

In Revelation 2:5, the Lord Jesus has given us a paradigm for the revitalization of a church, and it can be summarized by the three words *remember, repent,* and *recover.* But after we have remembered the past in celebration and repented of leadership sins, what exactly do we need to recover? Jesus called them the "first things," and they are what the rest of this book is about. As you read on, you will be reading about the strategies for church revitalization that God has provided for us in His Word. We must thoroughly understand these biblical dynamics and begin practicing them if we want to see any church become what the Lord meant it to be.

The first of the first things is the gospel of God's grace. That is where it all starts, and, by God's grace, that is where my revitalization ministry at Pinelands did start. Even before I preached my first sermon there, the challenges I was facing already seemed overwhelming. But I knew that there is power in the gospel (Rom. 1:16), and I suspected that some of the people in the church were unconverted, so I began by simply preaching the gospel. The text of my first sermon was 2 Timothy 1:12, from which I proclaimed the necessity and nature of personal saving faith in Christ. And through a series of amazing circumstances, starting with that message, over half of the congregation ended up making public commitments to Christ. Especially interesting are the stories of the church organist and a deacon, both of whom became true Christians that day, after years of involvement in the church. You will read of them in the next chapter.

QUESTIONS

1. Summarize the early history of the church at Ephesus. What was Jesus' plan for revitalizing that church in Revelation 2:5?

2. What do you think was good in the history of your church, and what do you think was bad?

3. What are some ways to celebrate and recover the good things that happened in the past, and what are some ways you could correct and repent of the bad things that happened?

4. Has the focus in your body been more on church growth or church health? What are some ways in which you could focus more on the health of your church?

5. How can the existing members be a "foundation" on which to build the future of the church, rather than a "scaffold" that is used temporarily and then discarded?

C H A P T E R

The Gospel of God's Grace

What do you preach for your first sermon at a new church when the Presbytery desires to close it down because it has declined from 960 attenders to under eighty? What do you preach when you have been told by a previous pastor that the mark of Satan is on the church? Where do you begin? In God's kind providence, the challenge I faced was clear. So I started with the gospel. My first sermon was drawn from 2 Timothy 1:12, where Paul says, "For this reason I also suffer these things, but I am not ashamed; for I know whom I have believed and I am convinced that He is able to guard what I have entrusted to Him until that day."

The message focused on the necessity of personal faith—Paul uses the word "I" six times in that one verse. I wanted my new congregation to know that saving faith consists of knowledge, conviction, and trust.[1] Paul says, "I *know,* I'm *convinced,* and I have *entrusted* myself to Him." Finally, I shared that our faith has only one proper object, which is Jesus Christ. "I know *whom* I have believed." Not *what, when,* or *that* I have believed. Paul did not put his confidence in his approbation of facts (what). He did not put his confidence in a conversion experience (when). He did not put his confidence in his faith (that). His confidence was rooted in the only proper object (whom), Jesus Christ—who He is and what He has done to save us from our sins.

I had arranged for the organist to come up after the sermon, while I was praying, and begin to play softly. I wanted to give people an opportunity to commit their lives to Christ right there. But as I began praying and encouraging the people to pray, I noticed that there was no music playing. I opened one eye and peered in the direction of the organ, only to find that no one was there. I was disconcerted, thinking that the organist should be there, especially because she was getting paid almost as much as I was! Then I thought that maybe my sermon was so bad that she had walked out! But as I swung my open eye back to the congregation, I saw that she was kneeling at the front of the church, with tears in her eyes and a smile on her face.

"Preacher," she said to me, "what you said, I don't have. I want that."

Her name was Roxanne. She was the head of the music department at Florida International University, and she had been the choir director at Pinelands for about eight years, but she didn't know Christ until that day. My wife counseled and prayed with her as we closed the service. Then I headed to the back of the church to greet people on their way out. But it was very strange. By the time I got to the back, there was no one left to greet. They had all beat me out of the church, and were pulling out of the parking lot when I stepped outside to look for them. I wanted to tell someone, "Thank you for coming, come back next week," but there was no one to tell. I had preached five minutes too long—that was one of the problems. And then there was that unprecedented conversion of the organist.

The chairman of the board of deacons found me, as he had stayed around for reasons of his own. "Harry, what was Roxanne doing down there today?" he asked me, with an expression on his face that I couldn't quite decipher.

"She was getting saved," I answered. "She gave her life to Jesus."

"I thought that was what was happening," he said, red-faced. I was afraid he was going to scold me for "rocking the boat" or introducing dangerous enthusiasms.

But instead, he said, "You know, I need to give my life to Jesus too."

"Well, Jack," I told him, "you don't have to come down to the front where Roxanne was. You can repent and believe anywhere you are. In fact, you can commit yourself to Jesus Christ right now and receive the gift of salvation right here."

"I knew you were going to say that," he smiled. "I did it right back in the pew when we were praying." Then his face turned sober again. "I've been a deacon here for fourteen years, and I have been a hypocrite. Can you let me come forward next Sunday at the end of the service so I can tell people that I am committing my life to Christ?"

I told him that we could arrange that, and then prayed with him before we went home.

On Thursday of that week, I got a phone call telling me that Jack had accidentally cut off his left thumb with a power saw, while he was making some furniture. They had rushed him to the hospital, and he was one of the first patients to benefit from the new microsurgical equipment that the hospital had just installed. The doctors had sewn his thumb back onto his hand, and they were hoping this new procedure would work. When I went to see him in the hospital, his hand was wrapped and immobilized up above his shoulder, to lessen the throbbing pain.

His first concern was whether he could come to church on Sunday and share his testimony with the congregation. I told him that was up to him and the doctors, but I also shared some principles from the Word with him. I explained that Satan was not happy about his new commitment to Christ, or his desire to share it with the church. I said that sometimes God allows Satan to attack us physically. But I also explained that there are two facts that he needed to realize. One, God is sovereign. Satan cannot do any more than God will allow him to do. Second, when God allows Satan to do something, it is always for a purpose, which is what we call the doctrine of divine providence. The Bible does not say that all things are good, but it does say that "God causes all things to work together for good to those who love God, to those who are called according to His purpose" (Rom. 8:28). So I encouraged Jack to trust in the Lord and have no fear.

On Sunday morning, he was in church, sitting in the back with his bandaged hand up in the air. So many times during the service I wanted to say "I see that hand," but I restrained myself. But at the end of the service, as we bowed for the closing prayer, Jack came walking down the aisle, hand in the air. I met him down in front of the pulpit and put my arm around him.

I told Jack that I didn't expect to see him there this morning, and he said, "Pastor, now that I know the gospel and what Jesus Christ has done for me, Satan could have taken my arm off at the shoulder and I would have been here today to tell others of my commitment to Christ. I have been a hypocrite for fourteen years, and today I want to make it right and let it be known that Christ is my Savior."

I then noticed that his lovely wife, Beth, had walked down the aisle and joined him there at the front. And then, as I stared unbelievingly, twenty-eight of the fifty-five people in the church ended up coming forward. They had all either committed their life to Christ for the first time or recommitted themselves to Him.

One message about the gospel of God's grace, and an unusual work of the sovereign hand of God, had begun a revival that would continue until that needy church had gone from embers to a flame. Even I, with all my weaknesses, could not have derailed this revitalization, because it was driven by the powerful engine of the gospel.

THE FIRST OF THE "FIRST THINGS"

That story illustrates the importance and effectiveness of putting the gospel first in a chronological sense—that is, at the beginning of your ministry to a group of people to whom you must be committed to preach and teach about God's grace in Jesus Christ. But we must also put the gospel first in other ways. It must be the *priority,* the *parameter,* and the *preeminent point* of our ministry, so that Christ will be exalted above all. The gospel of salvation by grace is the foundation, the formation, and the motivation for a "first love" church (and for the life of any individual Christian). We must build upon it,

57

allow it to determine the shape of all that we do for the Lord, and make sure that it is the reason why we serve Him. If the gospel is not central in the life of your church, you will never be successful in the eyes of the Lord.

The importance of God's message of grace is taught and illustrated everywhere in the Scriptures, but here are a few examples:

Titus 2:11–13. In verse 11 Paul says, "The grace of God has appeared, bringing salvation." Our salvation comes through the life of Jesus Christ and His death on our behalf, which was the living embodiment of God's mercy. This "past grace" must be understood and trusted for us to know God. But in verse 12 Paul adds that this grace is even now "instructing us to deny ungodliness and worldly desires and to live sensibly, righteously, and godly in this present age." We could call this "present grace," for it reveals not merely that we are *saved* by grace, but also that we must *live* by grace. And verse 13 says we should be "looking for the blessed hope and the appearing of the glory of our great God and Savior, Christ Jesus." There is a "future grace" that we must hope for and rely upon continually as a source of motivation in our service for the Lord.[2]

Romans 1:16 and 10:17. These two verses emphasize that it is only through the gospel that people can enter into a relationship with God. The first says, "I am not ashamed of the gospel, for it is the power of God for salvation." The second says, "Faith comes from hearing, and hearing by the word of Christ [*or literally,* the message about Christ]." But a closer look at Romans 1 reveals that Paul is speaking of the relevance of the gospel, not only for unbelievers, but also for Christians. According to Romans 1:15, Paul was "eager to preach the gospel to *you also* who are in Rome." Verse 7 identifies that audience as "all who are beloved of God in Rome, called as saints." In other words Paul wanted to preach to those who were *already saved,* the church. And do we not need to grow in faith even after we become Christians? So if faith comes from hearing the gospel, then we need to hear the gospel throughout our lives.

I used to preach the gospel to non-Christians, and then when they became believers, I would essentially put the gospel on the shelf and tell them everything they needed to do now that they were saved. But I realized along the way that such an approach was preventing them from real growth in Christ, because it was cutting them off from their greatest source of nourishment and strength. Now I would say that we can go deeper into the gospel, but we should never go beyond it. The message that unbelieving sinners need to hear is the same message that believing sinners need to hear. In other words, the gospel is for Christians too. We need to preach it to ourselves, each other, and the lost. We need gospel discipleship, along with gospel evangelism, to remain a Christ-centered church.

The book of Galatians. No book in the Bible emphasizes the importance of the gospel more than this letter of Paul. In Galatians 1:8, the apostle says, "But even though we, or an angel from heaven, should preach to you a gospel contrary to that which we have preached to you, let him be accursed." He repeats that statement in the next verse, and never uses language that strong regarding any other issue. In 2:2 he says that if he had gotten the gospel wrong, his entire ministry would have been "in vain." In 2:11 he says that he opposed Peter "to his face" because the other apostle was acting in a way that gave a wrong impression about the grace of God. In 5:4 he tells

59

those who have distorted the gospel that they have been "severed from Christ" and have "fallen from grace." And in 6:14 he summarizes all that he has said before: "May it never be that I should boast, except in the cross of our Lord Jesus Christ."

The gospel of grace is simply the most important factor in a ministry of revitalization, or in any other ministry of the Word. If you make it your primary focus and fight to keep less important issues from overshadowing it, you will see the hand of God at work in your midst.

In summary, the gospel of saving grace in Jesus Christ is an instrument that not only brings life to people who are dead in their sins, but also renews life where believers have faltered. The gospel is the gift of God for discipleship, as well as evangelism. And every text in the Bible, when understood in its context, points to the glorious truth of the gospel of grace in Jesus Christ. That's why the hearts of the disciples on the road to Emmaus burned within them when Jesus "explained to them the things concerning Himself in all the Scriptures" (Luke 24:27).

UNDERSTANDING THE GOSPEL OF GRACE

The gospel is the "good news" of God's salvation, which is offered to us in Christ. Most Christians know this, but many do not understand how comprehensive this salvation is. It is not merely a "ticket to heaven," but a package deal that includes much more than our eternal destiny. The gospel tells us about all the facets of God's salvation, so to be preachers of the gospel, we must remember and proclaim all of them. So here is a way of explaining the good news that I have found helpful. God's gracious salvation includes all of the following elements:

Salvation from the persuasion of sin—effectual calling. Second Thessalonians 2:14 says, "He called you through our gospel, that you may gain the glory of our Lord Jesus Christ." God's grace gives us eyes to see and ears to hear, where before we were by nature blind and deaf to the truth. I was raised in a church that preached the gospel, and I heard it over and over again. But it wasn't until I was twenty years old that suddenly it began making sense to me. I realized it was *I* who was a sinner, *I* who was headed for hell, *I* who needed to be forgiven. I also realized that Jesus had died for *me.* It was like the scales fell off, and it was because God was calling me by His grace.

Salvation from the power of sin—regeneration. This is what Jesus was referring to when he said, "Unless one is born again, he cannot see the kingdom of God" (John 3:3). Before we are born again, all we can do is sin. We are in slavery to it (John 8:34). We do not commit every possible sin, nor do we commit them in the worst way possible, because of the "common grace" that God has bestowed upon the world. But though we are not as bad as we could be in our unregenerate state, we still are incapable of doing anything truly good for the glory of God (cf. Isa. 64:6; 1 Cor. 10:31). But God is able to remove our hearts of stone and replace them with soft hearts, sensitive to His love and His leading (Ezek. 11:19; 36:26). And the result of this salvation from the power of sin is described in Romans 6:17–18: "Thanks be to God that though you were slaves of sin, you became obedient from the heart to that form of teaching to which you were committed, and having been freed from sin, you became slaves of righteousness."

That is the message that God has called us to proclaim. We are not preaching a self-help religion. We are not preaching Nike Christianity—"Just do it." If people could "just do it" in regard to their salvation, God wouldn't have sent His son. He would have sent a message that said, "Just do it—buck up, pull yourself up by your own bootstraps." But He sent His Son because we were dead in our sins (Eph. 2:1) and needed to be made alive in Him (Eph. 2:5). He gives us a new heart and a new nature so that we can repent and believe in Christ. Without that work of regeneration, we are lost—so we are utterly dependent upon His grace.

Somebody once asked me what I thought about Jessie Ventura's comment that Christianity is a crutch. "Jesse Ventura is wrong," I answered, which was no surprise to the person asking the question. But then I did surprise him when I said, "Christianity is not simply a crutch—Christianity is a *life-support system!*" Jesus did not come to give a helping hand to the weak or crippled—He came to give eternal life to the spiritually dead. That is why the new birth cannot be the reward of faith; it is a sovereign act of God, which enables us to believe.

Salvation from the penalty of sin—justification. When God imparts to us a new heart, He also imputes to us a new record. He declares us to be righteous in His sight, simply because Jesus Christ lived a perfect life and died a sacrificial death as our representative. When we believe, we receive His righteousness as a free gift of grace (Rom. 3:21–24; 6:23). We are clothed with Christ (Gal. 3:27) and forever cleansed of our sin, as Isaiah 1:18 says: "'Come now, and let us reason together,' says the LORD, 'though your sins are as scarlet, they will be as white as snow; though they are red like crimson, they will be like wool.'"

Everything in the gospel is "good news," but this has to be the best news of all!

Salvation from the position of sin—adoption. When God calls us by His Spirit, gives us a new heart, and declares us righteous before Him, He also brings us into a new family. Before, we were "children of wrath" (Eph. 2:3) and our spiritual father was the devil (John 8:44). But now God Himself has become our Father, for He has adopted us as His sons (Rom. 8:15; Eph. 1:5). So I am no longer an orphan of sin, but a child of the King! And as a child of the King, I am also an heir of all His kingdom promises (Gal. 4:6–7). I will be loving and serving my Father forever in heaven.

Salvation from the practice of sin—sanctification. The blessings of regeneration, justification, and adoption are granted to us in full when we become Christians. But the blessing of sanctification continues throughout our lives on this earth as God makes us more like Jesus by the progressive work of the Holy Spirit. In this sense, our salvation is still taking place. The Scriptures speak of "having been saved" in the past, but they also speak of "being saved" in the present (1 Cor. 1:18; 2 Cor. 2:15). Those verses are referring to the process of being sanctified, or "set apart" from sin. Ephesians 4:22–24 describes it this way:

> . . . that, in reference to your former manner of life, you lay aside the old self, which is being corrupted in accordance with the lusts of deceit, and that you be renewed in the spirit of your mind, and put on the new self, which in the likeness of God has been created in righteousness and holiness of the truth.

So the gospel is not just good news about how we can come to Christ for the first time, but it also tells us how we can walk with Christ for the rest of our lives.

Salvation from the presence of sin—glorification. One day the process of sanctification will be completed, and we will be given new bodies that are incapable of sin and pain (Rom. 8:23; 2 Cor. 5:1; Rev. 21:4). And in this sense our salvation is still future—that's why Paul can say that "now salvation is nearer to us than when we believed" (Rom. 13:11). We have been saved, we are being saved, and we will be saved—that is the good news that God wants us to proclaim as the foundation, formation, and motivation of all that we do in His church.

As you review the promises we have just discussed, you will notice that the gospel is entirely about *what God has done.* It is not about what we do. Even our sanctification is our working out what He is working within. Repentance from sin and faith in Christ are merely our response to the salvation that God freely offers to us. He does not save us because we decide to believe, but rather our faith is *the way in which He saves us.* That is why the Bible says that we are saved "through faith," and that faith itself is a gift of God's grace (John 6:65; Eph. 2:8; Phil. 1:29). So the gospel we preach must be one in which people are urged to trust in and rely upon Christ *alone* for their salvation—past, present, and future.

A good illustration of this came from a good old country boy named Buzz, who lived near Macon, Georgia. I shared the gospel with him over lunch one day, and as we finished eating he took the check in his hand, excited about what he had learned.

"My daddy raised me and told me that whenever I eat with a preacher, I should pick up the tab. So I am going to pay for lunch today," he told me.

"Buzz, you have a smart daddy," I said with a smile. "You do what your daddy tells you."

"Okay," he said, returning my smile. Then he added, "Now if I understand what you're telling me, Jesus came into the world two thousand years ago, and He picked up my tab. And what I need to do is receive what He offers me because He has paid for it, and stop trying to pay for it myself."

Buzz trusted Christ that day and served the Lord for the rest of his life. He got the point of the gospel, and it motivated him to follow Christ. Two years ago I stood beside Buzz's grave at his memorial service—he had an untimely death in his mid-forties. But I was able to tell over five hundred people there that day about God's saving grace in Buzz's life. His conversion, and even his home-going, became a tool that God used to bring the good news to many needy people.

When you focus on communicating this message of good news in your ministry, it will also provide people with the hope they need to face the hardest times. The last time I talked to Roxanne, the organist who became a Christian on my first Sunday at the church in Miami, was when she told me that she had terminal lung cancer.

"They say I don't have long," she said. "I think God is planning to take me home soon. But I'm ready, and I want to go to be with Him." Here was a woman who had sung with the Metropolitan Opera, directed a university music department, and had a long list of other accomplishments. But all she wanted to talk about at the end of her life was that Sunday morning when God changed her heart and life when she believed in Jesus Christ as her Savior. The salvation she had received that day was her most precious possession and all that consumed her as she stood on the edge of eternity. And that is what the gospel can do for anyone—it is truly "the power of God for salvation to every one who believes" (Rom. 1:16).

APPLYING THE GOSPEL OF GRACE IN YOUR CHURCH

Since the gospel is such an important, powerful, and life-changing message, it should be the center of everything we do in the church of Jesus Christ. All preaching and teaching must be related to the gospel, if not based on it. For example, if you teach about family worship, make sure that people understand *why* we should worship the God who gave Himself for us. And if you preach on a particular command of God, such as giving or sexual purity, talk about *how* we can truly obey—only through the grace of God that comes to us through the cross.

Every text of Scripture, in one way or another, is connected to the gospel. Find that connection and help your people to see it. Remember that the gospel is not only for unbelievers, but for Christians too. And realize that there are great depths of truth that can be mined from the promises of God. So to preach the gospel constantly does not mean that all your preaching will be "milk," rather than "meat" (see Heb. 5:12–14). The gospel needs to be in the "milk," but it also needs to be in the "meat." Or, to put it another way, we can go deeper into the gospel and apply it more widely, but we should never leave it.

What we must avoid at all costs is the kind of preaching and teaching that is mere moralism. Bryan Chappell explains this well:

> However well-intended and biblically rooted may be a sermon's instruction, if the message does not incorporate the motivation and enablement inherent in a proper apprehension of the work of Christ, the preacher proclaims mere Pharisaism. Preaching that is faithful to the whole of Scripture not only establishes God's requirements, but also highlights the redemptive truths that make holiness possible.[3]

Avoid Errors That Distort the Gospel

If Satan cannot get us to neglect the gospel, he will try to infect the gospel with disease and distortion. How might he do that?

All of the work of the gospel except sanctification is monergistic—God alone is working. Sanctification is synergistic in that God's people now have the dynamic of His Spirit enabling them to work with Him. Sanctification is God's work and yet we must cooperate. We are not passive. Satan seeks to distort our understanding of this in two directions.

Sometimes he tempts us to fall into an activism or moralism that views our activity as the key to our sanctification. Then, when we realize that we grow by the power of God working within us, not our own strength, we may slip into passivism, thinking that we should simply "let go and let God."

How do we avoid the extremes of activism and passivism? The gospel message is not that sanctification is 50 percent God and 50 percent me. It's not 100 percent God and 0 percent me. It is 100 percent God's power working within me, which I am totally dependent on, and 100 percent of my commitment and devotion to doing the things Scripture calls me to do, such as fleeing temptation, studying the Word, and pursuing holiness.

A similar way the gospel is distorted is by either legalism or licentiousness. We may think that our salvation is grounded in what we do. The truth is that we don't work for our salvation; we work for our Savior who has done the full work for our complete salvation. But when we realize that legalism is to be avoided, we may then adopt a libertine approach in which our careless thoughts, words, and deeds presumably prove how dependent we are upon God's grace. The Bible says no to this error as well. It tells us to walk in a manner worthy of our calling, to walk circumspectly as Christians.

Scripture constantly puts all of this together when it tells us not to *work for* our salvation but to *work out* our salvation. Why? Because "it is God who is at work in you, both to will and to work for His good pleasure" (Phil. 2:13). Paul instructs Timothy, "You therefore, my son, *be strong in the grace* that is in Christ Jesus" (2 Tim. 2:1). There is my responsibility in gospel discipleship: be strong, not *for* grace, but *in* the grace that is found in Christ Jesus. If I am in Christ Jesus, then I have God's grace at work in me and upon me. What I am doing is working out what He is working within. So Paul says, "I urge you therefore, brethren, by the mercies of God [not *for* the mercies of God], to present [not passively] your bodies a living and holy sacrifice, acceptable to God, which is your spiritual service of worship" (Rom. 12:1). Notice that all of life is to be an intentional, conscious statement of worship to God, not to pay back His grace, but to honor and adorn the grace of the gospel with our lives for the glory of God.

Our growth in grace does not make God love us more. Instead, knowing God's love makes us grow more. God loves us *in Christ*—not because of who we are or what we do, but because of who Christ is and what He has done. And since God will never stop loving Christ, He will never stop loving us! Nor will He ever love us more or less than He does right now—*in Christ.*

Think of someone who is a new Christian, perhaps one who is still struggling with serious problems like alcoholism or drug abuse. Now imagine that this person will go on to conquer his addictions, raise a godly family, become a successful pastor, and win thousands of people to Christ. What you need to remember is that the new, struggling believer will never be more called than he is right now. He will never be more born again than he is right now. He will never be more justified than he is right now. He will never be more adopted as a son of God than he is right now. He will hopefully grow to be more like Christ in his practical living, and he will also grow to enjoy his relationship with God more and more. He may also have to endure less discipline from his loving Father. But his Father cannot love him more than He already does in Christ.

If a church maintains a continual emphasis on the wonderful truth of God's free grace, it will not fall into the trap of legalism or moralism. Nor should it fall into the other extreme of licentiousness or antinomianism (opposition to the law). Emphasizing grace at the expense of obedience, the means of grace, or the pursuit of holiness has always been a serious danger to the church. Remember that the gospel tells us of salvation from the persuasion of sin, the power of sin, and the practice of sin. Jesus came not only so that we could be forgiven for our sins, but also so that we could be *changed* by the power of the Holy Spirit (Titus 2:11–14; 1 John 3:1–10).

In recent years, much of the church has been awakened to our need to preach the grace of God and to avoid "mere moralism." This is an encouraging development, so long as we do not adopt what I call a Bohemian view of grace. Liberation from legalism and moralism should not make it fashionable to prove how much we believe in grace by how close we live to sin. Remember, a deep, heartfelt belief in the grace of God should not lead us to sign peace treaties with sin. The grace of God does not lead us closer to sin, but farther away from it. So we should hate sin when we see how much it cost in the shedding of Christ's blood, when we see how heinous it is in the sight of God that it took His only Son to save us from it. And we should be so grateful for the grace of God in Christ, that we will want to obey Him and serve Him. Jesus said, "If you love Me, you will keep My commandments" (John 14:15).

The good news of grace and the call to repentance and commitment to Christ are not contradictory or exclusive of one another—when they are rightly understood. We should tell people that God loves them enough to forgive them right now, no matter how bad they may be. But we should also tell them that He loves them enough not to leave them the way they are. We must make it clear that the root of all good works is faith in Christ, but we must also insist that the root will always produce fruit. Or, to use Jesus' words mentioned above, we want to liberate them from the notion that God will be enabled to love them if they keep His commandments. But we also want them to know that if God loves them, they will love Him as a result, and will *want* to keep His commandments.[4]

So in order to see the power of the gospel at work in your church, you must present its truth in a biblical and balanced way. To paraphrase Martyn Lloyd-Jones: *If you are not vulnerable to the charge of antinomianism, then you have not preached the gospel of grace with clarity. But if you have not answered the charge of antinomianism, then you have not preached the gospel of grace with integrity.* This comes from Paul's words in Romans 6:1 and 6:15, where he implies that he has been criticized for making it too "easy" to become a Christian. The critics have been saying that Paul's doctrine of grace leads people into greater sin, because they know they will be forgiven freely by God on the basis of the work of Christ. But he answers the charge by using some of the strongest words in the Greek language (the maledictory oath *mē genoita,* translated "May it never be!"). And he proceeds to explain that someone who is truly saved by grace will be changed forever by that grace, so he or she will not want to live in sin anymore.

Ephesians 2:8–10 is also very helpful in this regard. There Paul says, "For by grace you have been saved through faith; and that not of yourselves, it is the gift of God; not as a result of works, that no one should boast. For we are His workmanship, created in Christ Jesus for good works, which God prepared beforehand, that we should walk in them." Picture it this way: The gospel is the river of life. The dam of legalism can stop it from flowing, and the toxic waste of antinomianism can pollute it. Ephesians 2:8–9 ("by grace you have been saved") blows up the dam of legalism, and then verse 10 ("created . . . for good works") cleans out the pollution of antinomianism. So we are left with a beautiful flood of God's grace, which is able to turn people away from both their self-righteousness and their self-absorption.

Praise God that His grace in Jesus Christ takes us right where we are, but never leaves us where we are—it changes us from faith to faith, victory unto victory, all the way to glory.

Focus on Jesus Christ, the Hero of the Gospel

A gospel-centered church is a Christ-centered church, because He is the embodiment of the good news. So, to emphasize the grace of God while avoiding those dangerous errors, we must build our ministries around the person of Jesus Christ. As Hebrews 12:1–2 says, "Let us run with endurance the race that is set before us, fixing our eyes on Jesus, the author and perfecter of faith."

How can we fix our eyes on Jesus, as a church in need of revitalization? All our preaching and teaching, as well as the ministries of the body, must be focused on Him. We must constantly emphasize the preeminence of Christ (Col. 1:17), the love of Christ (2 Cor. 5:14), the cross of Christ (1 Cor. 2:2), and the necessity of abiding in Christ (John 15:1–8). And, most

71

of all, we must always remember that the church belongs to Jesus Christ. It is not our church, and it does not belong to a denomination. It is the bride of Christ and the body of Christ.

In Matthew 16:18, our Lord Himself said, "I will build My church, and the gates of Hades shall not overpower it." In addition to making clear that the church belongs to Christ, that verse also gives us the confidence we need to carry on in a ministry that may be struggling. We are not the ones who build the church—it is Jesus who does that. We are merely called to labor under and alongside Him in this task. So, as we continue to work with Him, by trusting Him and following His instructions, the possibilities for this "construction project" are endless! A thousand talented and committed "experts" could not build or renew a church apart from Christ. But with Him, just one faithful man, no matter how weak or inadequate he may feel, can see it happen.

An old Civil War legend says that General Sherman's army was passing through a valley when they saw a lone Confederate soldier up on a hill, waving a rebel flag and taunting them. When Sherman sent three soldiers up the hill to get him, the graycoat disappeared over the hill and the Union soldiers disappeared too, following him. Sherman and the rest of his men heard the sounds of a battle over the hill, and soon the Confederate soldier appeared alone on the hill again, waving his flag. So this time Sherman sent a whole squad up to get him, and they all disappeared again, followed by the same noises. Once again the Southerner appeared alone on the hill, waving his flag. So Sherman said, "Take a whole battalion up there, and get that guy." The battalion proceeded up the hill, and chased the man over it. The ensuing skirmish was louder, and this time one Union soldier came crawling back over the hill to Sherman, wounded and shaking his head.

"Sir, don't send any more men after that soldier," the man pleaded.

"Why?" Sherman asked.

"Because it's a trap. There are two of them!"

That story illustrates the truth of the gospel, which can save your soul and also serve as the sure foundation for a successful church. In spiritual warfare, it only takes two to defeat all the armies of hell. You and Jesus Christ make an invincible team, and evil can never win as long as He is with you. He protects you from the judgment of hell, and He will protect you from the failure of a dying ministry. But He and His gospel must be the center of all you do, so that His power can work in you, and all the glory for your victories will go to Him.

QUESTIONS

1. Why is the gospel the *first* of the "first things" that a church needs to recover? What makes it so important in the ministry of the church?

2. Review the elements of the gospel discussed on pages 60–64. Which of these do you think should be emphasized more in your body?

3. What is the danger of legalism (or moralism), and how can it affect the church negatively?

4. What is the danger of licentiousness (or antinomianism), and how can it affect the church negatively?

5. Is your church a Christ-centered church? Why or why not? How could it become more Christ-centered?

The Role of Prayer

Most of us are aware of the difficulty of building a fire without a match or a lighter. We may have read the famous short story "To Build a Fire" or seen Tom Hanks struggle through endless attempts in the movie *Castaway*. Or perhaps we've experienced it ourselves as part of a scouting or camping program.

Now imagine that you have to start a fire in outer space. Try as you may, you will never be able to do it. (This may disappoint science fiction fans, but all those fiery explosions we see in space movies are actually more fiction than science!) And the reason there is no fire in space is that there is not enough oxygen to produce it.

When we desire to see our churches go from embers to a flame, prayer is the spiritual element that corresponds to oxygen in a fire. Without the oxygen of prayer to produce the flame of renewal, no amount of human effort can make it happen. In fact, the more we work at revitalization, the more frustrated we will become—unless our constant prayers are providing the spiritual spark we need.

THE PRIORITY OF PRAYER

If the first of the "first things" is the gospel of God's grace, then the second would have to be prayer. (Or, prayer may be tied for first.) And if there is anything that a dying church needs, it is prayer. The early church at Jerusalem was successful in every way imaginable (see Acts 2:43–47; 4:32–35), and there was no bigger reason than the fact that it was founded on prayer.

Consider the very beginning of the church, for instance. Before Jesus ascended to heaven, He told the disciples that the Holy Spirit would soon come upon them, and that they would be His witnesses to the world (Acts 1:4–8). So Acts 1:12–14 says:

> Then they returned to Jerusalem from the mount called Olivet, which is near Jerusalem, a Sabbath day's journey away. And when they had entered, they went up to the upper room, where they were staying. . . . These all with one mind were continually devoting themselves to prayer.

When they gathered in the upper room on the Day of Pentecost, some time later, we can assume that they were doing the same thing that they had been doing earlier. Presumably they had been praying together like that regularly, perhaps even daily. And on that particular day, the promised Spirit came upon them, three thousand believed and were baptized, and the church was formed (Acts 2:41). All this happened in response to faithful prayer.

Shortly after that, as the church developed, a crisis arose that threatened to distract the leaders of the church from this all-important ministry. Acts 6:1–4 records the story:

> Now at this time while the disciples were increasing in number, a complaint arose on the part of the Hellenistic Jews against the native Hebrews, because their widows were being overlooked in the daily serving of food. And the twelve summoned the congregation of the disciples and said, "It is not desirable for us to neglect the word of God in order to serve tables. But select from among you, brethren, seven men of good reputation, full of the Spirit and of wisdom, whom we may put in charge of this task. But *we will devote ourselves to prayer,* and to the ministry of the word."

Prayer was so important to the founders of the church, and so integral to its success, that they were determined not to be pulled away from it, even by other good and necessary ministries. But often in our churches today every other ministry takes priority over the ministry of prayer. And I would suggest that many times this is the primary reason why churches decline or die. They may have charismatic leaders or slick programs, but they have become ineffective because the church has stopped praying. On the other hand, any church that commits itself to prayer, no matter how bad things may have become, can be renewed and rebuilt by the power of the Spirit.

To do that, however, we need to know *how* to pray for revitalization in our churches, and in the Scriptures God has provided for us some model prayers that are especially relevant to this topic. So, in the rest of this chapter, I would like to discuss two such prayers, one from the Old Testament and one from the New.

REVISITING THE PRAYER OF JABEZ

First Chronicles 4:9–10 says,

> And Jabez was more honorable than his brothers, and his mother named him Jabez saying, "Because I bore him with pain." Now Jabez called on the God of Israel, saying, "Oh that Thou wouldst bless me indeed, and enlarge my border, and that Thy hand might be with me, and that Thou wouldst keep me from harm, that it may not pain me!" And God granted him what he requested.

About twelve years ago, I was introduced to this prayer by a friend and began to teach it. At the time, it was an obscure passage of Scripture, but it is not so obscure anymore! Several years ago, Bruce Wilkinson, of Walk Thru the Bible Ministries, published a little book called *The Prayer of Jabez*. The book has spent several years at the top of the best-seller lists, and it seems that almost everyone has now heard about this formerly unfamiliar Old Testament prayer. Since the publication of Wilkinson's original book, there have been numerous spin-offs, including *The Prayer of Jabez for Women, The Prayer of Jabez for Teens, The Prayer of Jabez for Kids, The Prayer of Jabez Devotional, The Prayer of Jabez Journal, The Prayer of Jabez Leather Edition,* not to mention a music CD, a portable MP3 player, T-shirts, hats, posters, coffee mugs, calendars, and even a mousepad.

Obviously many Christians have been blessed by the prayer of Jabez in recent years, but unfortunately many have also been turned off to it because of the glut of merchandise and because of some problems with Wilkinson's treatment of the passage.[1] For the first group—those who like the book—I want to point out some of those problems, so you won't be misled into any harmful error. But for the second group—those who do not like the book—I want to challenge you to remember that Jabez's prayer is *in the Bible* and therefore "inspired by God and profitable for teaching, for reproof, for correction, for training in righteousness" (2 Tim. 3:16). *Rightly understood,* the prayer recorded in 1 Chronicles 4:9–10 can be a helpful model for us, and it may be especially helpful in relation to church revitalization.

What's Wrong with The Prayer of Jabez?

In order to use the prayer of Jabez properly, it will help to understand how it has been misused. I am reluctant to criticize Bruce Wilkinson's book, because it has some good parts and has produced some good results (not the least of which is simply encouraging people to pray more). But it has enough issues that it needs a "warning label," if you will. If not read with careful discernment, its content can lead Christians down the wrong path. So consider the following concerns regarding *The Prayer of Jabez,* and hopefully they will lead us into a better understanding of the passage—and of prayer in general.

The first problem with Wilkinson's book is that *it wrongly identifies the "key" to Jabez's success.* In fact, it seems that Wilkinson builds the entire book (even an entire "industry") on a misconception. After wondering aloud why Jabez was so blessed by God, he says, "Clearly, the outcome can be traced to his prayer."[2] This is the assumption that lies behind everything said in the rest of the book—that the words spoken to God by Jabez were the key to his success. Later, the book refers to him as a man "whose prayer earned him a 'more honorable' award from God."[3]

I would suggest that Wilkinson has it backwards at this point. It is much more logical, and more consistent with the rest of Scripture, to understand that the key to Jabez's success is to be found in his character—in the fact that he "was more honorable than his brothers."[4] That statement comes first in the brief narrative, and it reflects a wealth of biblical teaching about the kind of man that God blesses. Here are a few examples, all related to prayer:

> For the LORD God is a sun and shield; the LORD gives grace and glory; no good thing does He withhold from *those who walk uprightly.* O LORD of hosts, how blessed is the man who trusts in Thee! (Ps. 84:11–12)

> The sacrifice of the wicked is an abomination to the LORD, but the prayer of the *upright* is His delight. (Prov. 15:8)

> The LORD is far from the wicked, but He hears the prayer of the *righteous.* (Prov. 15:29)

> O Lord, I beseech Thee, may Thine ear be attentive to the prayer of Thy servant and the prayer of Thy servants *who delight to revere Thy name,* and make Thy servant successful today, and grant him compassion before this man. (Neh. 1:11)

> The effective prayer of a *righteous* man can accomplish much. (James 5:16)[5]

If there was any key to Jabez's success, or to his prayers being answered, it was the fact that he trusted, worshiped, and obeyed God as a pattern in his life. And this godly character must have taken many years to develop—it was anything but a quick and easy route to the blessing of God.[6]

On the other hand, if Jabez had *not* been "more honorable than his brothers," his prayer would have meant nothing and would have yielded nothing from God. The psalmist says, "If I regard wickedness in my heart, the Lord will not hear" (Ps. 66:18), and Peter tells husbands to "live with your wives in an understanding way, . . . so that your prayers may not be hindered" (1 Peter 3:7). *The Prayer of Jabez* simply does not teach this clearly enough. In fact, because of the erroneous claim that the prayer was the key, and the lack of important qualifiers, the book can easily give the impression that God will answer this prayer regardless of the honor or righteousness that we possess by His grace.

Another problem with the book, and the whole Jabez marketing enterprise, is that *biblical prayers are models, not mantras.* God does not intend for us to "use" the prayers in Scripture in the way that people in Eastern religions repeat the same words over and over, as if they had some kind of magical power. Yet this is the impression given by Wilkinson, who says, "I prayed Jabez's prayer word for word" every day (p. 11). He says things like "I've been praying Jabez for half my life" (p. 16), refers to "Jabez prayers" (p. 71), speaks approvingly of those "who use the Jabez prayer" (p. 84), and challenges his readers to "start praying the Jabez prayer" (p. 87). All this makes it sound more like reciting a mantra than praying a biblical prayer.

There is no indication in 1 Chronicles, or anywhere else in Scripture, that Jabez or anyone else ever prayed these words

81

in any other setting, let alone repeated them over and over again. When Jabez prayed to God, he undoubtedly said many more words than those in the verse, and the ones recorded there are probably a summary, capturing the essence of his prayer. Therefore, we should seek to emulate the essence of this prayer, and other ones in the Bible, but we should not repeat the same words over and over again.

When Jesus gave the Lord's Prayer to His disciples as a model prayer, He did so after warning them about "meaningless repetition" (Matt. 6:7). Then He introduced the model prayer, not by saying "Repeat these words," but by saying "Pray, then, *in this way*" (v. 9). As one of Wilkinson's critics writes concerning the Lord's Prayer,

> There is absolutely no indication that our Savior ever intended even this archetype to be a prayer of repetition. We never, for instance, find Jesus leading His disciples in a recitation of this prayer. Nor do we find any mention of it in the New Testament church, the book of Acts, or the epistles. It clearly was never intended to be a prayer to be repeated verbatim; it was simply a model prayer, an example. The disciples asked Jesus to teach them how to pray, not to give them a prayer (Luke 11:1), and that is exactly what He did.[7]

I do not believe that it is wrong to recite the Lord's Prayer verbatim at times, but I do believe that most of our prayers should be personalized versions of that prayer and other biblical prayers, informed and governed by the principles of prayer taught throughout the Scriptures. When the *Prayer of Jabez* approach is taken, there is a danger that we might neglect the other model prayers, or that we might violate biblical principles of prayer in one way or another.

One such principle is that God often answers our prayers with a no, and He also often answers them in a way that is contrary to our desires (Matt. 26:39–42; 2 Cor. 12:8–9). And this leads to another major problem with the Jabez book: *it implies that the "blessing" of God will always be something we like.* The Bible says, "Blessed are those who *mourn*" (Matt. 5:4), and, "If you should *suffer* for the sake of righteousness, you are blessed" (1 Peter 3:14; cf. 4:14). But Wilkinson gives the impression that "praying Jabez" will get you what you want. He begins the book by saying, "I want to teach you how to pray a daring prayer that God always answers," and he apparently believes that the answer will always be yes. I say that because the book never discusses the possibility of unanswered prayer. Nor does it ever teach the important biblical truth that God knows better than we do, and therefore many times does *not* give us what we want, because it would be bad for us. All of Wilkinson's examples, on the other hand, are examples in which his desires were fulfilled. And he says repeatedly that the result of this prayer will be "miracles"— hardly a term that includes suffering and persecution! In this way *The Prayer of Jabez* unfortunately echoes some themes associated with the "prosperity gospel," as its critics have pointed out.[8]

The prayer recorded in 1 Chronicles 4 is part of a *narrative* portion of Scripture, and therefore must not be taken as *normative.* Jabez received what he wanted, by God's sovereign design, but that result cannot be expected by everyone who seeks it. In His infinite wisdom and love, God often blesses us by withholding the "blessings" we ask for. So the many testimonials of "answered" prayer in Wilkinson's book do not necessarily prove anything. There could be just as many testimonials of "unanswered" prayer, like the one displayed on a piece of clothing (an interesting addition to the parade of merchandise): "I prayed the prayer of Jabez for 30 days, and all I got was this lousy T-shirt!"

There are other problems with *The Prayer of Jabez*, including an implicit denial of the sovereignty of God.[9] But the concerns I have expressed should be a sufficient caution so that we can now consider a more correct understanding of the prayer.

What's Right with the Prayer of Jabez?

As I mentioned earlier, 1 Chronicles 4:9–10 is a part of Holy Scripture, so it is "inspired by God and profitable for teaching, for reproof, for correction, for training in righteousness; that the man of God may be adequate, equipped for every good work" (2 Tim. 3:16–17). So ignoring the prayer of Jabez, or saying that it does not apply to us, is an overreaction to the problems with the popular book. When it is rightly understood, the prayer of Jabez does apply to us, and it may even be especially applicable to the leaders and members of a church that needs revitalization.

Jabez came into the world at a hard time, and he even had a hard time coming into the world! He had everything stacked against him, both in the cultural context around him and in his own personal history.

By comparing the genealogies in the early chapters of 1 Chronicles, we learn that Jabez was born in Israel about five generations before David, during the time of the judges.[10] And the character of this period of Israel's history is made clear by a statement made twice in the book of Judges: "In those days there was no king in Israel; every man did what was right in his own eyes" (Judges 17:6; 21:25). Stories of brutal and senseless violence pervade the book of Judges precisely to make the point that these were bad times for Israel, both morally and culturally. So Jabez lived at a time when his people—his "church," if you will—were weak and hurting.

And his early life was filled with pain. In fact, pain wasn't just his middle name—it was his first name! First Chronicles 4:9 says, "His mother named him Jabez saying, 'Because I bore him with pain.'" Bruce Wilkinson explains this, and its implications, very well:

> In Hebrew, the word Jabez means "pain." A literal rendering could read, "He causes (or will cause) pain." Doesn't sound like the start of a promising life, does it?
>
> All babies arrive with a certain amount of pain, but something about Jabez's birth went beyond the usual—so much so that his mother chose to memorialize it in her son's name. Why? The pregnancy or the delivery may have been traumatic. Perhaps the baby was born breech. Or perhaps the mother's pain was emotional—maybe the child's father had abandoned her during the pregnancy, maybe he had died; maybe the family had fallen into such financial straits that the prospect of another mouth to feed brought only fear and worry.
>
> Only God knows for sure what caused the pain of this anguished mother. Not that it made much difference to young Jabez. He grew up with a name any boy would love to hate. Imagine if you had to go through childhood enduring the teasing of bullies, the daily reminders of your unwelcome arrival, and mocking questions like, "So, young man, what *was* your mother thinking?"
>
> Yet by far the heaviest burden of Jabez's name was how it defined his future. In Bible times, a man and his name were so intimately related that "to cut off the

85

name" of an individual amounted to the same thing as killing him. A name was often taken as a wish for or prophecy about a child's future. For example, Jacob can mean "grabber," a good one word biography for that scheming patriarch. Naomi and her husband named their two sons Mahlon and Chilion. Translation? "Puny" and "pining." And that was exactly what they were. Both of them died in early adulthood. Solomon means "peace," and sure enough, he became the first king of Israel to reign without going to war. A name that meant "pain" didn't bode well for Jabez's future.[11]

Despite all that Jabez had going against him, however, he became honorable and honored, and his prayers were answered by God. You may be in a church that seems to have everything going against it—pain and difficulty in the past, a wicked culture around you, and seemingly grim prospects for the future. But God blessed Jabez, and He is able to bless you, if you will ask him to do so through biblical and faithful prayer!

That is indeed what Jabez asked God: "Oh that Thou wouldst bless me indeed, and enlarge my border" (1 Chron. 4:10). Wilkinson's book says that Jabez was asking God for greater opportunities to serve Him and reach others for His glory. As his critics have pointed out, this is largely conjecture that cannot be proven from the text itself—Jabez may have actually "just wanted more land." But it seems clear that Jabez was a godly man, and therefore he would not have wanted the land for purely selfish reasons. And we know from elsewhere in Scripture that it is not wrong to ask God for what we want—in fact, we are encouraged to do so by command and example (see 1 Kings 3:5; Matt. 26:39; John 16:24). So we encounter an important truth in the prayer of Jabez: *We should ask God to bless us, even in the specific ways that we desire.*

For some reason, we tend to view such prayers as "self-ish" or "unspiritual," and so we might skip directly to "Your will be done" without ever telling God what *we* would like to see done. But if we have committed ourselves to Christ, and are walking in the Spirit, then we should ask Him for what we want, endeavoring to conform those prayers as closely as we can to God's revealed will. We should ask for revitalization in the church, we should ask for many people to be saved, we should ask for the funds to improve the facility, we should ask for leaders who will be a perfect fit for each ministry, we should ask for inroads into our particular community, and so on.

As you do this, remember that it is important to pray with an attitude of humility and submission, knowing that it may not be God's will to grant your requests. He may choose to bless you in some other way, even through trials and suffering. But you should bring your requests to Him, nonetheless. As was the case with Jabez, your desires may coincide with His gracious plan for your life. And then you will know the thrill of answered prayer, as your ministry grows for the glory of God!

Jabez did not pray only for blessing, however; he prayed also for *protection*. He asked "that Thy hand might be with me, and that Thou wouldst keep me from harm, that it may not pain me!" (1 Chron. 4:10). The Hebrew word translated "harm" can refer to sin itself, or to the consequences of sin. The word is often rendered "evil," so Jabez may be asking God for protection from the evil in himself or from the evil of others. And we know from elsewhere in Scripture that either request is a good one. The Lord's Prayer, of course, includes both when it says, "And do not lead us into temptation, but deliver us from evil [*or,* the Evil One]" (Matt. 6:13). The most likely interpretation of Jabez's words, however, is the second one, because of the last phrase of the verse: "that it may not pain me." The word "pain" is the same one that is used in verse 9. The play on words seems to indicate that Jabez was saying, "Please don't let the pain implied in my name come upon me."

This fits perfectly with what we learned in the first two chapters of this book about our relationship to the history of our church. We are not to *live* in the past (whether it was good or bad), but we are to *learn* from it for the sake of the future. So applying this to our prayers, we should ask God to protect the church from the evils that have come upon it in the past. Once they have been identified, we should pray for wisdom in dealing with each specific matter. Through such prayers, God will help us to learn from the mistakes that were made, and He can turn the pains of the past into fruit for the future.

You should also be praying constantly for protection from the new evils that may come upon your church. As God begins His work of revitalization, Satan will respond with his own work of deceit, division, and discouragement. I suggest that you make a list of every tactic the enemy might use to keep your church from growing, and pray through it on a regular basis. This "preemptive strike" of prayer will cripple the opposing forces before they can even begin their attack!

First Chronicles 4:9–10 ends with a statement that "God granted him what he requested." God answers prayer! He doesn't always answer the way we want Him to, but He *does* answer prayer that is offered according to His will (1 John 5:14–15). This is the message that has blessed and inspired so many through *The Prayer of Jabez,* and it is the message that you should be hearing through the prayer of Jabez. In fact, the passage ultimately provides a type of our Lord Jesus, who intercedes for us and is always blessed by receiving answers to His prayers because His requests are always in accordance with the will of God (Rom. 8:34; Heb. 4:14–15).

If you really believe that God promises to answer prayer through Christ, it should motivate you to make believing prayer one of the biggest priorities in your ministry. It should be one of the "first things" you emphasize on your church's road to recovery.

TROUBLE IN THE EARLY CHURCH

A New Testament prayer that is especially relevant to revitalization is found in Acts 4:23–31. In the events leading up to this prayer, the young church in Jerusalem faced its first major problem when Peter and John were arrested in the temple and then told by the Sanhedrin to stop preaching and teaching about Christ. The new believers had suddenly gone from "having favor with all the people" (Acts 2:47) to being unpopular with the powers that be. They could no longer obey Jesus' command to make disciples without the risk of imprisonment and execution. The disfavor of the establishment would also bring financial difficulty for many of them, plus the emotional pain of being rejected and misrepresented.

So what did they do when they hit hard times? *They prayed.* Acts 4:23–31 says:

> And when they had been released, they went to their own companions, and reported all that the chief priests and the elders had said to them. And when they heard this, they lifted their voices to God with one accord and said, "O Lord, it is Thou who didst make the heaven and the earth and the sea, and all that is in them, who by the Holy

Spirit, through the mouth of our father David Thy servant, didst say,

> 'Why did the Gentiles rage,
> And the peoples devise futile things?
> The kings of the earth took their stand,
> And the rulers were gathered together
> Against the Lord, and against His Christ.'

For truly in this city there were gathered together against Thy holy servant Jesus, whom Thou didst anoint, both Herod and Pontius Pilate, along with the Gentiles and the peoples of Israel, to do whatever Thy hand and Thy purpose predestined to occur. And now, Lord, take note of their threats, and grant that Thy bond-servants may speak Thy word with all confidence, while Thou dost extend Thy hand to heal, and signs and wonders take place through the name of Thy holy servant Jesus." And when they had prayed, the place where they had gathered together was shaken, and they were all filled with the Holy Spirit, and began to speak the word of God with boldness.

In this brief section of Scripture, we see this church go from trouble to triumph, with prayer as the primary catalyst for their revitalization. Although the cycle of decline and renewal in our churches will take place over longer periods of time, the principles here are still applicable. To go from embers to a flame, we must pray, and we must pray according to the model of this prayer, in which every word is inspired by God.[12]

The Priority of Praise

Given their situation, we might have expected the believers to bring their problems immediately to God, asking Him to intervene on their behalf. But they did not actually mention their requests until the end of the prayer. They began by telling God how great He is. They said, "O Lord, it is Thou who didst make the heaven and the earth and the sea, and all that is in them" (v. 24). This is what we call praise, of course, and it is an appropriate place for all our prayers to start. By orienting our minds to the greatness of our God, we are then better able to pray according to His will and to have the confidence that this great God can indeed grant our requests.

Notice also that these prayers of praise are permeated by *Scripture.* Verse 24 contains a compilation of Old Testament verses, and verses 25–26 contain quotes from Psalm 2. One of the best ways to assure that we are praying according to the will of God is to use the words that are actually contained in His revealed will. This is a lost key to prayer, to be sure, but one that can unlock great power in your life and ministry. James Boice explains the connection between the Word and prayer:

> Prayer is our talking to God; the Scriptures are God's talking to us, and the two always go together. You pray in a right way when you pray scripturally. You study the Scriptures in a right way when you study prayerfully. This is what the church was doing. They had been reflecting on the Scriptures. Now, as they began to pray, the Scriptures rose up in them, and they found themselves talking to God in God's own words.[13]

I would suggest that you identify some Bible passages that relate especially to church revitalization, such as those discussed in this book, and begin to use them as a guide in your private and public prayers. As you talk to God in His own words, you will be praying more and more according to His will, and He will be answering those prayers more and more.

Prayer and Predestination

The believers in Jerusalem went on to say, "For truly in this city there were gathered together against Thy holy servant Jesus, whom Thou didst anoint, both Herod and Pontius Pilate, along with the Gentiles and the peoples of Israel, *to do whatever Thy hand and Thy purpose predestined to occur*" (vv. 27–28). It may seem strange to some that predestination is actually mentioned in a prayer, because to them predestination and prayer appear to be mutually exclusive concepts. If God has predestined everything, they say, why should we bother to pray? But this was not a problem for the early church; as one commentator says, they actually "found comfort in the fact that he knew beforehand what would happen."[14]

That is why the prayer begins with a reference to God as "Lord" (v. 24, Greek *despotēs*). As John Stott writes, "The Sanhedrin might utter warnings, threats and prohibitions, and try to silence the church, but their authority was subject to a higher authority still, and the edicts of men cannot overturn the decrees of God."[15] And they not only found comfort in the fact that God is in control, but also found motivation to pray, strange as that may seem. They knew that the same God who predestines has also chosen to accomplish His sovereign will *through* prayer, not apart from it. Put another way, the purpose of prayer is not for us to change the plan of God, but for us to participate in that plan. God graciously enables us to pray so that He can graciously allow us to be a part of His work in the world.

In his book *If God Already Knows, Why Pray?* Douglas Kelly explains this in a discussion of "Thy kingdom come, Thy will be done," from the Lord's Prayer:

> Jesus is telling us that our prayers are part of the outworking of [God's] purposes! We are given a mandate to become involved in His divine plan through our human praying. He invites us to approach Him with earthly needs, just like Jabez or those who prayed against the Spanish *Armada*. Our prayer can be effective in seeing that the divine "will is done."
>
> If this were not so, God would simply tell us that His kingdom will come, that we are not to worry. All that we would have to do would be simply to obey His revealed will and not pray for it! But in some extraordinary way, the unchanging, sovereign God, with an eternally defined purpose for His creatures, invites our input into the making of history.
>
> As we think about praying for the plan of God to come to pass in our lives and in the whole world, we can keep the right perspective if we hold together in our minds these two tremendous, Biblical truths. The first is that God has an all-encompassing plan and is utterly sovereign over all. The other is that human prayer really is effective in the supernatural realm.[16]

The sovereignty of God pervades this prayer in Acts 4—the members of the early church obviously believed in it deeply. Such a terrible event as the murder of our Lord by ungodly men is mentioned in their praise to God, because they recognized that He has a good purpose in even the bad things that happen. In light of this, let me ask you a tough question about your prayer life. Have you been able to praise God for the difficult situation you find yourself in? Or for the bad things that have happened in the history of your church? Have you been able to thank Him for giving you this challenge so that you might rely on Him fully and know that any good results come from Him alone? If not, then perhaps you are not yet ready to bring your requests to Him.

Pleadings and Petitions

The believers in Acts 4 had a deep, abiding trust in the sovereignty of God, and so they were prepared to pray according to His will and to see Him work through their prayers. Their first request was that God would restrain or remove their enemies ("Take note of their threats"), and their second was "Grant that Thy bond-servants may speak Thy word with all confidence" (v. 29). This was specific prayer, tailored to their specific situation, and, as we discussed earlier, it was what they wanted to see happen. Finally, they even had the audacity to ask God for healing and other miracles to accompany their ministry (v. 30). Whether we should ask for the same types of miracles today is a debated issue, but anyone on either side of that question can agree that, like the early Christians, we should ask God to do great things in our lives and ministries. If we ask for anything less, we sell God short, as if He were not "able to do exceeding abundantly beyond all that we ask or think" (Eph. 3:20).

So I suggest that you make another list, one that contains all the great things that God could do in and through your church as it is revitalized by the power of the Spirit. Begin praying diligently about every blessing that you can possibly imagine, and then watch as God does *more* than you can even imagine!

PRAYER WORKS?

The results of the early church's prayer are recorded in Acts 4:31: "And when they had prayed, the place where they had gathered together was shaken, and they were all filled with the Holy Spirit, and began to speak the word of God with boldness." God gave them a sign, and He gave them boldness—exactly what they had asked Him for. He also went beyond what they could ask or think by enabling them to love and care for one another in a way that amazed and impacted the world around them (vv. 32–37).

Because of the results of Jabez's prayer, the prayers of the early church, and many others like them, Christians have often been given to say, "Prayer works!" That is true, in a way, but in light of what we have learned in this chapter, it would be better to say, *"God works through prayer!"* The power that is at work belongs to Him, of course, not to the prayers themselves. But if you want to see that awesome power at work in revitalizing your church, you must pray.

You must not only pray, however, but also preach and teach the Word. Acts 6:4 says that the apostles devoted themselves "to prayer, *and to the ministry of the word.*" In the next chapter, you will learn how a church can be revitalized when godly men fight the devil with the sword of the Spirit.

QUESTIONS

1. If the prayer ministry of a church is the "thermometer" that measures its health, as Charles Spurgeon said, then how healthy is your church?

2. What errors should we be careful to avoid in our prayers, as illustrated by the book *The Prayer of Jabez*?

3. What principles from Jabez's prayer can be helpful in a ministry of revitalization?

4. Do you use the Scriptures themselves in your prayers? Name some different types of prayer, and list some passages that you could use for each.

5. Discuss the relationship between predestination and prayer. Are the two concepts antithetical to each other?

The Ministry of the Word

The church in Jerusalem was conceived in a prayer ministry (Acts 1) and birthed in a sermon (Acts 2). The apostles provided the model for all church leadership, especially pastors, when they said, "We will devote ourselves to prayer, and to the ministry of the Word" (Acts 6:4). In the previous chapter, we learned about prayer, and in this one we will discuss the other "first thing" mentioned in that verse: the ministry of the Word.

The early church in Jerusalem was highly successful, by any standard, and one of the biggest reasons was that the Word of God was the foundation for all they did as a body. For example, Acts 2:42 summarizes the activities of the church: "And they were continually devoting themselves to the apostles' teaching and to fellowship, to the breaking of bread and to prayer."

The fact that "the apostles' teaching" is mentioned first in that verse seems to indicate its importance, but it is also true that the other activities mentioned find their foundation and motivation in the ministry of the Word. The apostles' teaching is the Word *proclaimed,* of course, but we could also say that their fellowship was the ministry of the Word *shared,* that the breaking of bread was the ministry of the Word *visualized,* and that prayer was the ministry of the Word *returned.* Everything that they did as a church revolved around the Bible, and their devotion to it was a major key to their success. This applies to our churches today as well, and especially to those that are in need of revitalization.

In chapter 3, we learned that Timothy, a young pastor who served as Paul's apprentice, was involved in a ministry of revitalization at Ephesus (1 Tim. 1:3), and thus the entire book of 1 Timothy can be considered and studied as a textbook on this topic. In that book, Paul explains to Timothy how the Lord can use him to effect positive change in a church that has been declining. So it is interesting to note the high priority that 1 Timothy places on the ministry of the Word.

In 1:3–11, Paul starts the book by charging Timothy to "instruct" those who are promoting false doctrines, helping him to be able to distinguish between the right and wrong kinds of teaching in the church. In 2:11–12, Paul addresses the importance of women receiving instruction, rather than giving it to the men in the church. In 3:1–7, he encourages men to aspire to the office of elder, which is a teaching role, and lays down qualifications for those who will be ministering the Word in that way. The entirety of chapter 4 is given to another discussion of false teaching, and how to overcome it with the faithful ministry of the Word—and so on (see 5:17–18; 6:3–5, 17–21).

By the time Paul wrote his second letter to Timothy, which was probably the last book he wrote before his death, Timothy may still have been involved in his revitalization ministry at Ephesus, or perhaps at other churches as well. And 2 Timothy contains the same preponderance of passages about the ministry of the Word and its central role in all church work. The climax of the book, in fact, is a series of nine verses where Paul gives his final charge to Timothy, and all nine verses are about the preaching and teaching of the Scriptures. In 2 Timothy 3:1–13, Paul describes the incessant pattern of decline that will plague churches "in the last days," and he then provides the answer to such decline in his final charge. Second Timothy 3:14–17 tells us about *the message* that must be preached, and 4:1–5 describes *the man* who must preach the message.

THE MESSAGE PREACHED

Paul says in 2 Timothy 3:14–17,

You, however, continue in the things you have learned and become convinced of, knowing from whom you have learned them; and that from childhood you have known the sacred writings which are able to give you the wisdom that leads to salvation through faith which is in Christ Jesus. All Scripture is inspired by God and profitable for teaching, for reproof, for correction, for training in righteousness; that the man of God may be adequate, equipped for every good work.

99

What is the message that we must preach, if we are to see revitalization take place in the church? In this passage, the message that revitalizes is described in seven different ways.

A Gospel Message

First, we must preach the good news of salvation. Paul tells Timothy to remember what he has learned, saying, "From childhood you have known the sacred writings which are able to give you the wisdom that leads to salvation through faith which is in Christ Jesus" (v. 15). Paul's first concern about preaching was that it would be focused on the gospel of God's salvation and on the Scriptures that teach it. But notice what part of the Scriptures he is referring to. As a child, Timothy's Bible was the Old Testament! None of the New Testament books had been written yet! So this confirms what we discussed in the last chapter, that *all* of the Bible is gospel-centered, and that *all* of our preaching should therefore be gospel-centered.

According to Paul, even the Old Testament Scriptures are able to make us wise unto salvation. The gospel is not as clear in the Old Testament, but it is definitely there. Throughout its pages, the covenant of God's grace is being unfolded until it finds its fulfillment in Jesus Christ. And the message is the same in the Old as in the New—abandon all confidence in your own righteousness and trust in the mercy of God in Christ. So when we preach the Word, both the New Testament and the Old Testament, we must relate the passage to the gospel, or else we will not be "handling accurately the word of truth" (2 Tim. 2:15).

A Christ-Centered Message

Second, our preaching must focus on the person and work of Jesus Christ. Paul says that the Scriptures, both the

Old and New Testaments, are about "salvation through faith *which is in Christ Jesus*" (3:15). All of human history revolves around Jesus Christ, and everything in the Bible is about Him, in one way or another. The Creation took place so that God's plan of redemption in Christ could be enacted on the stage of a fallen world; the promises to the patriarchs find their fulfillment in Christ; the Exodus is a picture of salvation in Christ; the law was given to Israel so that it would be "our tutor to lead us to Christ" (Gal. 3:24); the repeated failures of the kings of Israel and Judah are recorded so that we might see the perfection and majesty of the one true King; the prophets foretold His coming; and so forth.

The Gospels record His works and His words, Acts describes the building of His church, and the Epistles finish His revelation to us and point us back to Him as the only source of salvation. So if a sermon does not tell us something about the person and work of Christ, it has failed to capture the meaning and purpose of the text it is expounding. And it has failed to fulfill the meaning and purpose of preaching itself. That's why many pulpits have traditionally been inscribed with the words "We would see Jesus." Let Him reveal Himself to His people when the Word is opened among them.

A God-Given Message

As Paul continues exhorting Timothy to be a preacher of the Word, he says, "All Scripture is inspired by God" (3:16). He wants his apprentice to understand that the purpose of preaching is not to communicate our own ideas, or even the ideas of great teachers who have gone before us. The purpose of preaching is to communicate *the words of God Himself.* So when we have an opportunity to preach or teach, the goal of our preparation and presentation should be to *say what God has said,* as faithfully and accurately as possible. If we are studying a particular passage of Scripture, we should aim to reflect the meaning, purpose, and outline of that passage—rather than imposing our own agendas or emphases on the text. And if we are presenting a topical message, our intention should be to communicate what God has to say about that topic, by pulling together the meaning, purposes, and emphases from various Scriptures. Biblical preaching is not having something we want to say, and then finding some verses to support it. It is speaking *for God,* and allowing Him to speak through us.

This approach to preaching and teaching is commonly called "expository," and that is a good term if it is understood to mean that we are "exposing" or "revealing" the meaning of the Word. For preaching and teaching to be expository in that sense does not mean that it has to be a series of sequential passages from a book in the Bible ("topical" studies can be expository in that sense), but it does mean that we must be allowing the inspired Word itself to dictate what we will say and how we will say it.

It was this kind of preaching that R. L. Dabney was speaking of when he urged "that the expository method . . . be restored to the equal place that it held in the primitive and Reformed Churches; for, first, this is obviously the only natural and efficient way to do that which is the sole legitimate end of preaching, convey the whole message of God to the people."[1]

And John MacArthur offers this paean of praise to the kind of preaching that proceeds directly from the Scriptures:

> Expository preaching—expressing exactly the will of the glorious Sovereign—allows God to speak, not man.
> Expository preaching—retaining the thoughts of the Spirit—brings the preacher into direct and continual

contact with the mind of the Holy Spirit who authored Scripture.

Expository preaching frees the preacher to proclaim all the revelation of God, producing a ministry of wholeness and integrity.

Expository preaching promotes biblical literacy, yielding rich knowledge of redemptive truths.

Expository preaching carries ultimate divine authority, rendering the very voice of God.

Expository preaching transforms the preacher, leading to transformed congregations.[2]

A Profitable Message

When preaching and teaching proceed from the inspired Word of God and communicate what God has to say, they are always "profitable," as the apostle Paul adds in verse 16. God's thoughts and ideas have divine power, with which they can grip hearts and change lives, regardless of the weaknesses of the person presenting them.

Recently I was asked to preach at a conference for young college students. When it comes to "connecting" with the culture and preferences of people that age, I don't have the slightest idea. If you asked me who is the hot music group right now, for instance, I would probably say Hootie and the Blowfish (whoever they are). Let's face it—a man in his fifties is out of it! But I simply explained the meaning of a passage of Scripture and applied it to these young people as faithfully as I could. And to my surprise they listened, and they really seemed to like it! Many of them said afterwards that God had used it in their lives. Why did this happen? It was not because the preacher was so good, or the sermon so well crafted, but because it was the Word of God. The Word has the ability to "connect" with anyone anywhere, because it is written by the One who created all of us and knows us better than we know ourselves.

A Life-Transforming Message

God also knows what each person needs, better than any preacher or teacher. So when we faithfully represent what He has to say, lives are changed by the Holy Spirit. Second Timothy 3:16 says that the Word is "profitable for teaching, for reproof, for correction, for training in righteousness."

The order of the list in that verse, I believe, is significant. You cannot make application to the lives of people until you have first taught them what the Scripture says and what it means by what it says. But it is also not enough simply to explain the text—you must also apply it. And that application begins with "reproof"—people need to know where they have gone wrong. We are all sinners by nature, and we cannot change until we recognize our sins and realize that we need to change. But then the application should continue with "correction." That is the positive side of reproof—how we can make right what we have done wrong. And finally, no application is complete without "training in righteousness." Your preaching and teaching should help people to understand how to *practice* the things they are learning—not just in a moment of repentance, but in their ongoing, everyday lives as well.

The Word of God provides this model of instruction and application for us over and over again. One excellent example is the book of Ephesians. The first three chapters of that book contain discussions of the wonderful blessings we have in Christ (election, justification, the church, etc.). Then the next three chapters tell us how we should live for Christ. First we learn who we are in Christ, and then we learn who we should be for Christ. Ephesians 4:20–24 summarizes this by saying,

> But you did not learn Christ in this way, if indeed you have heard Him and have been taught in Him, just as truth is in Jesus, that, in reference to your former manner of life, you lay aside the old self, which is being corrupted in accordance with the lusts of deceit, and that you be renewed in the spirit of your mind, and put on the new self, which in the likeness of God has been created in righteousness and holiness of the truth.

So the great preacher Paul tells the Ephesians that it is not good enough to know only what Christ has done for them; they also need to know what they should do for Christ. And he is not content merely to state this general truth—he goes on in verses 25–32 to give specific, practical examples of what it means to "put off and put on":

> Therefore, laying aside falsehood, speak truth, each one of you, with his neighbor, for we are members of one another. Be angry, and yet do not sin; do not let the sun go down on your anger, and do not give the devil an opportunity. Let him who steals steal no longer; but rather let him labor, performing with his own hands what is good, in order that he may have something to share with him who has need. Let no unwholesome word proceed from your mouth, but only such a word as is good for edification according to the need of the moment, that it may give grace to those who hear. And do not grieve the Holy Spirit of God, by whom you were sealed for the day of redemption. Let all bitterness and wrath and anger and clamor and slander be put away from you, along with all malice. And be kind to one

another, tender-hearted, forgiving each other, just as God
in Christ also has forgiven you.

You can see from those passages that the apostle Paul is
an inspired example of a man whose ministry included all the
elements of teaching, reproof, correction, and training in righteousness. And that is the example we should be following as
we seek to bring about change in our churches and in the lives
of individual believers.

An Equipping Message

In 2 Timothy 3:17, Paul states the purpose for the preaching and teaching of God's Word: "that the man of God may be
adequate, equipped for every good work." Within the church,
Paul is saying, our preaching and teaching should primarily
be for the purpose of equipping or building up the saints, so
that they can be better worshipers and servants of God. Ephesians 4:11–12 reflects this emphasis when it says that Christ
has given "some as pastors and teachers, for the equipping of
the saints for the work of service, to the building up of the
body of Christ."

These passages can help us with one of the most con-
troversial issues in the church today: Do we focus on ministering to believers in our worship services or on reaching out
to nonbelievers? We certainly should be sensitive to the needs
of nonbelievers and careful not to offend them unnecessar-
ily (cf. Ps. 96:9–10; 1 Cor. 14:23–25). But the biblical model
is that the church should gather to worship and scatter to
evangelize, as the old saying goes. Our services should be
focused primarily on encouraging, strengthening, and training Christians, so that they can then take the gospel to those
who need to hear it.

If you focus your preaching and teaching primarily on nonbelievers, you run the risk of having an undernourished church. You may have more people coming in the front door, but they may also end up going out the back door before long, when they have not been sufficiently discipled and strengthened in the faith. This unfortunate dynamic is illustrated in a recent book entitled *Exit Interviews,* by William Hendricks. The back cover of the book reads:

> There's a dark side to recent reports of surging church attendance in North America. While countless "unchurched" people may be flocking in the front door of the church, a steady stream of the "churched" is flowing quietly out the back. It's estimated that 53,000 people leave churches every week and never come back![3]

G. A. Pritchard recently conducted a two-year, in-residence study of a well-known "seeker" church, where the stated purpose of the weekend services is to reach out to "unchurched Harry." Pritchard observed many good things in the church, but he also discovered an unfortunate trend that he calls "the problem of churched Larry." He found out that there are thousands of people who attend the weekend services and claim to be Christians, but have no other contact with the church or its ministries. Pritchard writes:

> "Ben," a staff member, explains how the weekend service itself hampers these churched Larrys from growing in the Christian life:
>
> > The philosophy of the church in some ways hinders that. . . . It's the danger side of reaching out to unchurched Harry and holding him and

encompassing him and meeting some of his needs
and making him feel comfortable and all that, and
even letting him continue to be anonymous.

Ben explains that this approach of "let's help them
out and lure them into having an interest in Christ" often
creates a situation where churched Larrys are given only
milk and remain spiritual babies.[4]

The Lord has graciously allowed me to have three very
different pastorates, and I have discovered in all of them that
it is not necessary to be seeker-centered in order to experience
numerical growth. It is good to be seeker-sensitive, it seems to
me, but a church that is seeker-centered is not biblically ori-
ented. In fact, when people ask me, "Do you have a seeker
church?" I usually reply, "I hope so, because all of our people
should be going out to seek and save the lost, like Jesus did."
When believers are continually strengthened in the Word, they
will be "seekers" themselves, carrying the gospel to a needy
world and bringing others in to learn the exciting truths that
they are learning.

A Sufficient Message

Finally, Paul says that biblical preaching and teaching is
enough to make believers *"adequate,* equipped for *every good
work."* The Bible contains everything we need for life and godliness (2 Peter 1:3), and we must be careful not to go beyond
"what is written" for our answers to the spiritual issues we face
(1 Cor. 4:6; cf. Mark 7:6–13). The Greek word translated "adequate" in 2 Timothy 3:17 can also mean "perfect," as reflected
in John Calvin's comments on this verse:

> Perfect means here a blameless person, one in whom
> there is nothing defective; for he asserts absolutely, that
> the Scripture is sufficient for perfection. Accordingly, he
> who is not satisfied with Scripture desires to be wiser
> than is either proper or desirable.[5]

Many preachers and teachers think they are being clever
and relevant by feeding the flock a diet of ideas from sources
like the ancient philosophers, popular psychologists, or contemporary social critics. They give the impression that we must
improve upon the simple or outdated principles of the Bible
if we are really to make an impact on people. But "professing
to be wise, they became fools" (Rom. 1:22), because, as God
says in Jeremiah 2:13, "They have forsaken Me, the fountain
of living waters, to hew for themselves cisterns, broken cisterns, that can hold no water." All truth is God's truth, but
God's Word is all truth, so every assertion of truth must be
based on the Word of God and tested by it. Only the inspired
Word of God has the ability to change the hearts of people,
and only the inspired Word of God is sufficient to meet all of
their deepest needs.

THE MAN PREACHING

After describing the message that we must preach in the
context of church revitalization, Paul continues by discussing
the kind of man who should be proclaiming this message.
(Remember that there are no chapter breaks in the original
text of Scripture.) Second Timothy 4:1–5 says:

> I solemnly charge you in the presence of God and of
> Christ Jesus, who is to judge the living and the dead, and
> by His appearing and His kingdom: preach the word; be

ready in season and out of season; reprove, rebuke, exhort, with great patience and instruction. For the time will come when they will not endure sound doctrine; but wanting to have their ears tickled, they will accumulate for themselves teachers in accordance to their own desires; and will turn away their ears from the truth, and will turn aside to myths. But you, be sober in all things, endure hardship, do the work of an evangelist, fulfill your ministry.

The man of God lives and speaks in the presence of God. Paul tells Timothy, "I solemnly charge you in the presence of God." Any man who would lead God's people must recognize the presence of God in his life and work. Particularly when a man steps into the pulpit, he must be conscious of the presence of God. Most of us who are pastors are very conscious of the congregation—we want them to listen, to understand, and to grow from their experience in church. But are we thinking about God? Are we concerned with *His* experience during that hour? We should be, because He is the primary reason we are there. And we should be seeking His approval more than anyone else's.

Have you noticed how people refer to the singing in church as "the worship time," as if the other parts of the service are not part of our worship? This is troubling, because Christians should recognize that prayer, saying the creeds, giving, and especially the sermon, are *all* part of our worship of God. But I wonder if one of the reasons why people do not know this is that preachers have forgotten to worship God when they preach. We may deliver carefully crafted sermons, but if we ourselves are not worshiping God when we do, then that element will be lost on the people as well. On the other hand, when we are preaching primarily for the glory and pleasure of God, we can draw the rest of the congregation into worship with us. In fact, that is just what the best preaching does.

The man of God lives and speaks in light of the return of Christ. At the beginning of his charge to Timothy, Paul mentions "Christ Jesus, who is to judge the living and the dead." And he adds that this charge is given "by His appearing and His kingdom." The second coming of Christ was on Paul's mind as he conducted his ministry, and he wanted it to be on Timothy's mind as well. Likewise, when we preach today, we should hear the footsteps of Jesus approaching. We should realize that He could come before we finish that sermon. We should hear the gavel of the Judge that will consign our listeners to an eternity in heaven or in hell. And we must remember that our message has the power to rescue them from ruin on that fearsome day.

The man of God is diligent in preparation. Paul tells Timothy to "preach the word; be ready in season and out of season." The Greek word for "ready" can be translated as "diligent" (KJV), but even if it means "ready," it still speaks of the need for diligent preparation. A man cannot be ready to preach at all times and in all situations unless he is a constant and faithful student of the Word. As John Stott writes,

> Expository preaching is a most exacting discipline. Perhaps that is why it is so rare. Only those will undertake it who are prepared to follow the example of the apostles and say, "It is not right that we should give up preaching the Word of God to serve tables. . . . We will devote ourselves to prayer and to the ministry of the Word"

(Acts 6:2, 4). The systematic preaching of the Word is impossible without the systematic study of it. It will not be enough to skim through a few verses in daily Bible reading, nor to study a passage only when we have to preach from it. No. We must daily soak ourselves in the Scriptures. We must not just study, as through a microscope, the linguistic minutiae of a few verses, but take our telescope and scan the wide expanses of God's Word, assimilating its grand theme of divine sovereignty in the redemption of mankind. "It is blessed," wrote C. H. Spurgeon, "to eat into the very soul of the Bible until, at last, you come to talk in Scriptural language, and your spirit is flavoured with the words of the Lord, so that your blood is Bibline and the very essence of the Bible flows from you."[6]

The man of God is determined and patient. The man who preaches or teaches God's Word must "reprove, rebuke, exhort, with great patience and instruction." This ministry requires a holy determination and an extra dose of patience, because many times we have to tell people what they do not want to hear. We must commit ourselves to speaking the words of God, regardless of how we think the people might respond. And we must *persevere* in speaking the words of God, over the long haul, because this passage promises us that there *will* be many temptations to discouragement. "The time will come when they will not endure sound doctrine," the apostle says. We must never give up, however, if we want one day to hear those blessed words from the Lord: "Well done, good and faithful servant" (Matt. 25:21 NKJV).

The man of God is serious about his work. Second Timothy 4:5 says, "Be sober in all things." It is interesting to note that in the Gospels a wide range of emotions are attributed to Jesus—sorrow, anger, joy, grief, etc. But not once are we told that He laughed. I think it is very likely that He did laugh at times, and He certainly exhibited a sense of humor in some of his teaching (straining a gnat and swallowing a camel, logs protruding from someone's eye, etc.). I'm sure His tongue was firmly planted in His cheek when He said things like that. But He was clearly not a comedian. I very much doubt that anyone would have known Him as a "fun guy."

Our Lord is a model for us in this, as He is in everything. We who preach and teach the Word of God are in a serious business. It is life or death, heaven or hell. What would you think of an emergency room doctor who constantly had the whole staff in stitches as he went about his work? Well, we are doctors of the soul, and the people we treat are all spiritually diseased in one way or another. Many are terminally ill, in fact. So even though I think humor has a place in our preaching and teaching (as it did with Christ), I don't believe it should be a prominent feature.

The man of God is focused and purposed in ministry. Paul concludes his charge to Timothy by saying, "Endure hardship, do the work of an evangelist, fulfill your ministry." I serve on the boards of two seminaries, so I talk to many young men who are preparing for the ministry. And I have often heard them say something like this: "I'm not sure what will fulfill me in ministry." My response is that they should be more concerned with fulfilling their ministry than being fulfilled in their ministry. The difference is crucial, because it is a difference between a focus on self and a focus on others. It is a difference between being motivated by our own goals and being motivated by the purposes of God.

It is interesting that Paul refers to the preacher or teacher as a "man of God" (3:17), because preaching and teaching truly is "a man's job." It is not a job for wimps, weaklings, or lazy people. We must endure much difficulty, we must be proactive and zealous in reaching out to the lost, and we must commit ourselves to "fulfill" the full scope of responsibilities with which God has filled our ministry. Paul was that kind of man, who faced even his imminent death with a brave resolve: "For I am already being poured out as a drink offering, and the time of my departure has come" (4:6). Nothing less than that kind of focus and purpose will bring us the satisfaction that Paul describes in the next two verses (7–8): "I have fought the good fight, I have finished the course, I have kept the faith; in the future there is laid up for me the crown of righteousness, which the Lord, the righteous Judge, will award to me on that day; and not only to me, but also to all who have loved His appearing."

The Role of Church Officers in the Ministry of the Word

For a church to go from embers to a flame, God's message must be preached and taught by gifted and qualified men. But for that to happen, these men (especially the pastor) must have the *time* to pray, study, and prepare. And this makes the ministry of elders and deacons indispensable. In Acts 6, when the apostles say that they must devote themselves "to prayer, and to the ministry of the word," their solution for meeting the other needs of the church was to ordain godly men who would be responsible for them (see vv. 1–6). Men like these became known as "deacons" (1 Tim. 3:8), and their role was to meet various needs in the church so that godly shepherds could devote themselves to prayer and the Word. Apparently some elders also had a similar function, because 1 Timothy 5:17 implies that not all elders "work hard at preaching and teaching." That is why the Presbyterian Church has both "teaching elders" and "ruling elders."

But whatever the governmental structure may be in your church, the important point to understand is that the ministry of the Word cannot flourish and bring new life to the body unless those who preach and teach have the time to prepare. So a leadership structure must be in place that can "free up" the pastor, especially, to do the hard work necessary for this ministry. So many pastors are forced to be a jack-of-all-trades and master of none. They are the worship leader, the music coordinator, the children's ministry organizer, the primary evangelist, the counselor, the arbitrator, the advertiser, the accountant, the janitor, etc. And they are still expected to produce profound and life-changing sermons on a weekly basis! Pastors usually have big hearts and are willing to do all those things, but are those the *best* things they should be doing with their time?

Ruling elders, deacons, and other leaders in the church need to step up to the plate and fulfill their ministry, so the pastor can fulfill his. Most men need to spend about fifteen hours in preparation for a good sermon, and ten more if they preach a second time that week. Then there are Bible studies, men's groups, and other opportunities for them to minister the Word. For a pastor to achieve excellence in this task, a lot of time is needed for study and prayer.

If you are an elder or a deacon, prayerfully consider how you and your church can make more time available for your pastor to pray and study. And if you are a pastor, continue on to the next chapter, so you can learn how to develop the kind of leadership that will assist you in this way.

QUESTIONS

1. Discuss the importance of good preaching and teaching in the local church. How are the other activities of the church related to it and affected by it?

2. Review the descriptions of the biblical message we are called to preach (pages 99–109). How would you evaluate the teaching ministry of your church in light of them?

3. Review the descriptions of the man of God on pages 109–14, and evaluate yourself in light of them. What areas of weakness do you need to work on, and how do you plan to do so?

Leadership Multiplication

Leadership works. I am convinced of it.

"Harry, what about bad leadership?" you might ask.

It works also. I know there are some bad leaders, but even bad leadership works—it just doesn't produce the right results. Good leadership leads people the right way, and bad leadership leads people the wrong way—but either way, people are being led. Jesus said it this way: "A disciple is not above his teacher, nor a slave above his master" (Matt. 10:24). He also commented specifically on bad leadership: "If a blind man guides a blind man, both will fall into a pit" (Matt. 15:14).

Leaders have such an impact on people, in fact, that a church cannot be revitalized without good ones. But unfortunately there is a dearth of good leadership in our day.

WHERE ARE THE GOOD LEADERS?

In the America of the past, the church defined leadership for the rest of the country and produced many of the country's leaders. Men and women who were trained to lead in the church overflowed into other parts of society, such as the business world and the government. And the current of that flow from the church to the world was so powerful that even non-Christian leaders would adopt the Christian concept and methods of leadership. Thus, a pure deist like Benjamin Franklin, who didn't believe in prayer, would stop the Constitutional Congress and call for prayer. He did so because he had observed what effective Christian leaders did, and Christian leaders always stopped to pray. In this way and many others, the church used to set the pace for leadership in our world.

Today, however, it is a different story. The church does not define leadership for the society any longer, nor do we produce leaders for the society. We are not even producing a sufficient number of good leaders for the church itself, let alone enough to overflow into the world. On the contrary, many churches today are taking leaders that the world has produced to fit their standards, and trying to turn them into elders and deacons in a three-week officer-training class.

We have to reverse that process. We have to again define leadership for the world and develop leaders. And we have to deploy leaders not only in the church, but also in the business community, government, schools, guilds, the arts, the entertainment industry, and so on. If we do not produce godly leaders for those positions in the church and in society, they will most surely be filled by ungodly leaders. Nature abhors a vacuum.

For your church to go from embers to a flame, you need to develop leaders, and then deploy them in the church and in the society around you. You will have to do this intentionally, purposefully, and with a lot of hard work. Good leaders don't just appear out of thin air—they must be raised up, trained, and tested. But when they are, their lives and ministries will bear abundant fruit for the glory of God, in the church and throughout the world.

What Is Good Leadership?

The kind of leadership we need in the church can be defined briefly by three maxims. First, good leaders learn from the past, but they don't live in it, as we discussed in chapter 2. Second, good leaders live in the present, but they don't accommodate to it. In this way, they are "thermostats" rather than "thermometers." Thermometers merely reflect the environment around them, whereas thermostats change the environment. And third, good leaders look to the future, but they don't wait for it.

Another way to define a leader is by what he or she does. A leader *influences others to effectively achieve a defined mission together.* What follows is a discussion of each part of that definition, which will paint a picture of the kind of leader you should be, and also the kind of leaders that you want to produce in your church.

The Influence of Godly Leaders

Leadership, by definition, means influence. But for it to be a truly good influence, it must be one that comes from God and points others to God. So how does the godly leader influence others to become more godly?

119

Education. In the most important verse in Scripture about leadership development, the apostle Paul tells his apprentice, "The things which you have heard from me in the presence of many witnesses, these entrust to faithful men, who will be able to teach others also" (2 Tim. 2:2). Paul had taught Timothy what Scripture says, what it means by what it says, and how it applies to life and ministry. And he never stopped teaching, because people learn by instruction.

I lived in Charlotte, North Carolina, for many years, and had the opportunity to see a lot of college basketball. When I watched Duke and North Carolina play, one thing that always fascinated me was that Mike Krzyzewski and Dean Smith never stopped coaching. Even if their teams were forty points ahead, or behind late in the game with no chance of winning, these great coaches would still be elbowing the guy next to them, or moving back and forth in front of the bench, giving pointers about the sport. Obviously their goal was not just to win the game, but also to teach their players something at all times.

In the same way, good leaders in the church will always be teaching others about the ways of God. That is why Paul also told Timothy, "Preach the word; be ready *in season and out of season;* reprove, rebuke, exhort, with great patience and instruction" (2 Tim. 4:2).

Embodiment. Good leaders also influence others by personally embodying the truths that they teach. People learn by imitation. My observation over the years leads me to agree with the saying that most of what we learn is *caught* rather than *taught.* In other words, we learn as much or more by imitation as we do by instruction. The instruction is crucial, certainly, but it cannot produce the desired results if people don't also have a model they can follow. Paul said, "Be imitators of me, just as I also am of Christ" (1 Cor. 11:1). He told Timothy, "Let no one look down on your youthfulness, but rather in speech, conduct, love, faith and purity, show yourself an example of those who believe" (1 Tim. 4:12). So as a leader, you should be one who embodies the characteristics that you are hoping to produce in others. And you should also point people to other godly men and women who are worthy of imitation. People will always have heroes, and you have an opportunity to lead them toward some good ones, instead of the immoral "celebrities" who are so esteemed by the world. Celebrities live off the culture as parasites; heroes are those who have changed the culture and are assets to society.

Many of the best heroes are men and women from past eras. People living today, however impressive they may be, have not yet "finished the course," so the jury is still out on them to some degree. I remember in the 1970s when both President Jimmy Carter and Governor Ronald Reagan had their pictures taken with a pastor in San Francisco who was supposed to be a model of urban ministry and racial reconciliation. Both men would have liked to take that picture back, because a little while later that man, Jim Jones, led 914 people into mass suicide in Guyana, South America. We will not have any problems like that with godly people who lived in the past, because their chapters of history have already been written.

Empowerment. Those who influence others not only embody the truths they teach, but also empower others to succeed. Inspiration and motivation are their "stock in trade." One such leader was Douglas MacArthur.

During World War I, MacArthur was a brigadier general. His brigade, entrenched in France, was given the responsibility of taking an enemy position that had already repulsed

121

three American attacks and inflicted heavy casualties. MacArthur divided his troops into three wings for the assault, and planned to lead the middle wing himself. But he realized that the left flank was the weakest, so before the charge he went over to talk to the major leading those troops. The general said, "Son, I want you to take that position over there. It is seventy yards away. Other men have tried and haven't made it. But I know that you are going to make it. When you finish, I am going to see to it that you get one of these." He showed the young major a medal of bravery he had received earlier in the war from the French. Then he turned around and walked away.

When he was about ten yards away, he suddenly turned around and walked back to the man. "Son, I *know* you are going to get there," MacArthur said, pulling the medal back out and handing it to the major. "So you go ahead and take mine now."

Do you think that young man was empowered? Do you think he sensed that his leader really believed that he could get the job done? We can show the same confidence in those we are training for leadership, because we have a God who "is able to make all grace abound to you, that always having all sufficiency in everything, you may have an abundance for every good deed" (2 Cor. 9:8).

Evaluation. Finally, those who influence others must stay connected, so they can affirm what has been done well and identify the areas that need improvement. A good leader does not have the luxury of watching his people do the job without coming back into their life to celebrate, affirm, and evaluate their work. This shows that the leader is concerned not only with the mission, but also for the people involved in it.

The Effectiveness of Godly Leaders

A leader is one, we said, who influences others to *effectively* achieve a defined mission. One way of describing the effectiveness of a good leader is to say that he, and those who follow him, learn to do the right things in the right way at the right time for the right reasons.

A leader knows how to do the right things. Busyness alone is no guarantee of effectiveness. In fact most of us are too busy and can't say no. You will never be able to say no until you have a bigger yes. We must be busy doing the right things. I once heard someone in the corporate world say, "You can be the most efficient ladder climber in the world, but if you don't have the ladder against the right wall, it won't do you any good."

That illustration and the following are adapted from the book *First Things First,* by Covey, Merrill, and Merrill:[1] Imagine that someone is teaching about time management in a classroom setting. He pulls out a large jar, and in that jar are a number of big rocks all the way to the top. Another big rock sits on the table beside the jar. The teacher asks if the jar is full. The students say yes, and the teacher shakes the jar and makes room for one more big rock. He asks again if the jar is full, and the students say yes. He reaches down underneath the table and pulls out a jar of gravel that he pours in and it filters down through the big rocks and fills to the top. He then asks the students if they think the jar is full now. This time some of them say no, because they are catching on. The teacher reaches under the table again and brings out a jar of sand, which he then pours over the gravel. It fills to the top. Once again the teacher asks the students if they think the jar is full. They all say no because they figure there must be another jar—and there is. The teacher reaches under the table and pulls out a jar of water.

He pours it into the rocks, gravel, and sand, until it fills the rest of the space left in the jar. The teacher then asks the students what they have learned from this experience. Most of the students say that they have learned a lesson about time management—that there is always room to squeeze in a little more. The real message is not primarily about time management, however, but about self-management. "The point," says the teacher, "is that the big rocks must go in first."

What are the big rocks in your life? Like the teacher's rocks, you can never squeeze them in after everything else. They must go in first. Your calendar is like that jar—you have to put the big rocks (priorities) on it before anything else. Then if you have to say no, you will be saying no to the gravel and sand, instead of the most important things.

An effective leader knows not only how to do the right things, but also how to do the right things in the right way. He knows how to achieve goals with excellence. He wants to hear those blessed words from Jesus someday: "Well done, good and faithful servant" (Matt. 25:21, 23 NKJV). I know that motivates me to do what I do with excellence. I do not want to hear "mediocre," or "average," but "Well done!" And I believe that that commendation will be based on the "talents" that God has given to me, not on a comparison with others (see the parable in Matthew 25). So I do not expect to hear Jesus say, "Harry, you are the best preacher that ever lived." But I want to be the best preacher that Harry can be. I want to be the best leader that Harry can be. I want to maximize my potential before the Lord. And you, too, should want to hear from the Lord, "Well done. You did the right things, and you did them well."

Good leaders also do the right things at the right time, and they do them for the right reasons. This last mark of effectiveness is so important for a Christian leader because God is as concerned with our motivations as He is with the results, if not more. And our first motivation should always be for His glory and pleasure. First Corinthians 10:31 says, "Whatever you do, do all to the glory of God." And 2 Corinthians 5:9 says, "Therefore also we have as our ambition, whether at home or absent, to be pleasing to Him."

But we should also be motivated more for the good of others, rather than ourselves. The greatest leaders have always been concerned first with the people who follow them. General Robert E. Lee was an example of this, when the surrender at Appomattox was approaching, and his defeated army of fewer than 25,000 men begged him to let them form up for one more charge against the Union Army of 145,000. He said to them, "No, men, it is over," and then he added, "I have done the best for you that I could." At the surrender meetings, he asked for only two concessions from the Union generals, and they were both for the benefit of his troops. He did not even mention himself or his interests in the proceedings.

I cannot stress enough that you must lead, and train others to lead, for the glory of God and the good of others. It will eventually become apparent, in one way or another, if you are driven by a prideful desire to be admired, well known, powerful, or successful in any worldly sense. People can tell whether you have genuine motives or whether you merely want to use them to achieve your own ends. And good people will follow you to the ends of the earth if your heart is pure.

The Legacy of Godly Leaders
The third key word in the definition of leadership is "together." A good leader influences others to effectively achieve a defined mission *together*. This is the main point of this chap-

ter, and the main point of all leadership. A leader is not someone who does all the ministry in a church, but someone who attracts, develops, and deploys others to do the ministry with him. Or, in the words of Ephesians 4:11–12, God has given leaders to the church "for the equipping of the saints for the work of service, to the building up of the body of Christ." To put it yet another way, leaders must be reproducing themselves in the body if the body is to remain healthy. This happens when leaders work together with others in the body.

In the book *The Leadership Engine* Noel Tichy offers some great insight into effective business leadership that I believe also applies to church ministry. In his study of successful institutions, he noticed not only that they position proven leaders, but that those leaders intentionally and continually reproduce themselves at every level of the organization.[2] In other words, if you are a leader, anything you do by yourself is a waste of time. But if you do your ministry with someone else, then everything you do becomes discipleship and leadership training. You are not only ministering, but also instructing and providing a model to imitate. You are constantly reproducing yourself at every level of God's organization.

If you and I die, or move on from our present ministry, and we do not have other leaders trained and ready to take our place, then we have not been good leaders. Period. The truest test of a leader is not simply the success of his mission, or the number of his followers, but the number of others whom he attracts, develops, empowers, and enables to be leaders. Great leaders develop more leaders; they multiply themselves continually and intentionally. And one of the primary ways they do so is through *delegation*.

Sometimes there is a need for a strong, authoritative style of leadership, such as when there is an emergency and someone has to be decisive. I have a pastor friend whose community was devastated by a hurricane, and at that time he told me, "Harry, one thing about this is great. I am a 'high D' personality, and I don't have to apologize for it. Everybody is glad, because they want somebody to make a decision." An authoritative style is appreciated at a time like that; if a ship is sinking, it's not the time to call a meeting and confer. In that kind of situation, a good leader will take the reins and make things happen, all by himself if he has to.

But in most normal circumstances, a delegatory leadership style is better than an authoritative one. The leader who delegates or shares leadership responsibility will find that the gifts of other leaders complement his, producing greater success in ministry. If you train and involve others in the ministry that you do, they will be ready to step up to the plate when you are absent or unable to fulfill a particular responsibility. And if you have to leave the church at some point, the ministry will go on undaunted through the leaders you have raised up.

The only man in the history of basketball who was able to hold Michael Jordan under twenty points per game was Dean Smith, his college coach at North Carolina. Jordan scored fewer than twenty points per game there because Smith forced him to pass rather than shoot all the time. But in retrospect, Jordan has said that learning to pass was the greatest lesson he ever learned—one that was indispensable on his road to six NBA World Championships. Jordan also learned to celebrate after he scored by pointing to the player who had passed him the ball. So by sharing the work, and sharing the glory, he became the greatest ever. Likewise, when we minister *together* with other leaders, we can achieve true success.

Working together with other leaders will often eliminate the kind of divisiveness that can occur between strong personalities in the church. When we join together to fight a common battle, we tend to overlook our differences more easily, like politicians who put aside their disagreements at a time of national crisis. After the terrorist attacks of September 11, 2001, political opponents joined hands to sing "God Bless America" on the steps of the Capitol. That kind of unity can be developed and sustained in the church, but to do so we have to remember that we are on the same side in a battle with the forces of darkness, and that we need every hand manning the guns.

Pastor or church leader, if you want to train and deploy an army of ministers in your church, you will have to swallow your pride and get rid of any selfishness that might keep you from sharing responsibilities in the body. My daughter Abigail illustrated this truth in a beautiful way a few years ago when she ran in a six-mile race that was part of her training for the Olympic trials. There were two ex-Olympians in the race as well, and before it started, she and I were discussing how great it would be if she would win it. It was just a training race, but to finish before two famous runners would certainly make her daddy proud!

As the long-distance race eventually drew to a close, I was amazed to see that Abigail was in the lead! There was no doubt that she would win it if she kept up the same pace. But as she approached the finish line, she slowed down intentionally. Other runners passed her, including both of the famous ones. Finally, a girl from her team caught up to her. Abigail took her hand, and finished the race together with her. When I asked Abigail about it, she said, "It was not a competitive race, and my friend has been struggling lately. I thought if she finished alongside of me, it would be encouraging for her."

I learned a lesson from my daughter that day. In some ways, she was more mature than I was. I wouldn't even let my kids beat me at H-O-R-S-E, if I could help it! But she wanted to see that girl succeed, even though that meant less glory for herself. That is the kind of leadership I want to have. I may finish first, or I may not finish first. But I want to finish strong, and I want to bring some others with me. That is what good leaders do.

PROFILE OF A MULTIPLICATION LEADER

The test of a leader is not the breadth of his or her following but the quality of leaders he or she multiplies by attracting, refining, developing, and discipling. What would a "multiplication leader" look like? The following five traits are adapted from Noel Tichy's discussion in *The Leadership Engine*, for the purpose of multiplying church leadership:[3]

1. A multiplication leader is a learner. Once you quit learning, you forfeit the opportunity to teach, lead, and coach others.
2. A multiplication leader seizes on learning moments, which come not so much in prosperity as in adversity. Such moments are the greatest opportunities for learning. Our Lord used challenges, adversity, and failure to ring the school bell and teach us to grow as leaders. Scripture says, "Consider it all joy, my brethren, when you encounter various trials, *knowing that the testing of your faith produces endurance*" (James 1:2–3).
3. A multiplication leader is always teaching and coaching others. As mentioned earlier, basketball coaches like Dean Smith and Mike Krzyzewski never stop coaching, no matter what the score. As a result they produce not only many players who move on to the NBA, but also

many coaches who in turn coach others on the high school, college, and professional levels.

4. A multiplication leader always helps others to seize their personal learning moments. Because such learning moments often come in adversity, this presents a challenge if you are a pastor. You want to comfort people in times of trouble. But while you have your arm around someone, you may need to give him a good, swift kick and say, "You have a lot invested right now, and the Lord is teaching you something. The Lord is refining you and chipping off the rough edges. These are your learning moments. Learn from them now so that you won't have to go through this again."

5. A multiplication leader uses teaching maxims. He learns to put ideas in clear, memorable terms that people can hold on to and practice. These maxims or aphorisms need to provide a vivid connection between principles and their application as people are growing. As people practice these maxims and pass them on to others, they imitate the example of the multiplication leader.

Of course, the above traits are useless unless they are patterned after *the* great multiplication leader, Jesus. He was a learner: "And Jesus kept increasing in wisdom and stature, and in favor with God and men" (Luke 2:52). He seized adversity as His personal learning moments: "Although He was a Son, He learned obedience from the things which He suffered" (Heb. 5:8). Jesus was a continual teacher and coach. It is no small thing that people called him Rabbi or teacher.

Jesus was a master at helping His disciples seize personal learning moments. When did He teach Peter? When the disciple was sinking in the ocean, and when Peter failed and denied Him. And look at how Jesus used teaching maxims—His parables and illustrations and memorable sayings—so that even today we remember things like "It is more blessed to give than to receive" and many others sayings we recall in times of difficulty.

A Curriculum for Leadership Development

How can you multiply leaders who are influential, effective, and able to produce more leaders for the glory of God? I want to suggest a basic outline you can follow as you plan and personalize the leadership training in your church. The three sections correspond to the three parts of Hebrews 13:7, which says, "Remember those who led you, who spoke the word of God to you; and considering the result of their conduct, imitate their faith."

That verse is directed to followers, but it reveals some important things about leadership. First, it describes "those who led you," showing that the people who had authority in the church knew how to lead in an effective manner. Second, those leaders "spoke the word of God"—they had enough knowledge of the Scriptures that they were able to teach others. And third, their conduct was worth imitating.

The basic outline I am suggesting for a leadership curriculum reflects these three emphases, but reverses their order in accordance with the relative importance of each. As you train leaders for the church, you should be training them in the aspects of *character, content,* and *competency.*

Character

One of the reasons that training should start with character is the nature of the qualifications for a leader listed in

131

1 Timothy 3. Fifteen of the seventeen qualifications pertain to character and conduct, whereas only two relate to skills. Paul says that they must be able to manage and able to teach, but the other qualifications are all about the kind of person a leader should be. This indicates to me that character is even more important than knowledge and competency, and that the latter two flow from the first.

I have known pastors who could ace any theological examination and blow away anyone else in a doctrinal debate. But they destroy every church they are in because they lack character. On the other hand, I have known men of character who are not the epitome of intellectual prowess, by any means. But one of two things happens as they continue in ministry: either they become more adequate through a lot of hard work, or they surround themselves with others who can make up for their weaknesses.

It is interesting to notice what kind of people a leader surrounds himself with. Some are only interested in surrounding themselves with people who will make them look good. But the best leaders want the kind of help that will be good for the people under their care, because that is their primary concern. They are not in this to massage their egos, but to minister to others. So they are even willing to be "upstaged" by other leaders if that will serve the people better.

If you are to raise up the kind of leadership that can take a church from embers to a flame, you will have to identify and train people who have that kind of humility, as well as leadership skills. If they have the leadership skills, but no character, they will be using their abilities to manipulate others for their own ends. But godly character and conduct provide the appropriate foundation to teach leadership skills that will be used with integrity to minister for the benefit of God's people.

George Washington Carver was an example of the kind of selfless leadership we need today:

> During the Great War Thomas Edison secretly offered Carver a job at a salary variously reported as $100,000 per year, $200,000, or five times the salary of the President of the United States.... In *Success* magazine, Carver said of the offer, "There was nothing to talk over, and I thanked Mr. Edison in a letter." Carver made it clear that he would rather stay among "his people" in the South and help them improve themselves.[4]

It was rumored that Carver received a similar offer from Henry Ford later in his life, but again he refused. During all this time, he continued teaching and training "his people" at the Tuskegee Institute in Alabama, making far less money than was involved in those offers. He simply was guided not by greed, but by calling, and by the needs of the people he served. That is character.

Likewise, Robert E. Lee was inundated with many attractive financial proposals after the Civil War was over. A New York firm offered him $50,000 a year to promote trade with the South. The Knickerbocker Insurance Company offered him $25,000 a year to be its president. But Lee ascertained that those job offers were based on his fame and not his resident skills, so he graciously turned them down, saying that he had to work for his wages. It would not be right, Lee said, to profit from his fame in light of the great sacrifice by so many associated with it. In addition, he refused the offer of a British nobleman who promised an estate plus $15,000 a year. After thanking the admirer, he declared, "I must abide the fortunes and share the fate of my people." And perhaps the most telling feature of his character was the refusal of an offer from a Northern life insurance company, which promised $10,000 simply for the use of his name. He graciously declined, informing his would-be benefactor, "My name is not for sale at any price."

Instead, Lee ended up serving as the president of Washington College for $1,500 a year because, like Carver, he wanted to give the rest of his life to the education of young people.[5]

Another anecdote from the life of Robert E. Lee illustrates one of the most important truths for a potential leader to learn: *Circumstances do not dictate our character. Instead, they reveal it and provide the opportunity to refine it.* A good leader does not use bad circumstances as an excuse, but as an opportunity for great things to happen by God's grace.

In May 1865, General Lee had just surrendered at Appomattox. The following Sunday, as was his custom, he attended the worship service at St. Paul's Episcopal Church. Like most churches in the South, this one had segregated seating for worship. The former slaves were in the balcony; the whites were on the ground floor. When the Lord's Supper was administered, the white congregation would walk down first to partake of it, while the black congregation sang hymns. Then the whites would sing while the blacks took communion. On this particular day, however, when the Lord's Supper commenced, two Union soldiers brought a freed slave down the aisle to receive the Supper, at the time usually reserved for the white congregation. The church fell absolutely silent at this brazen protest of their tradition, for it was clear that the soldiers were more concerned with creating an event than worshiping God. The tense silence continued for a moment, until measured steps were heard on the marble walkway on the side of the sanctuary. Robert E. Lee made his way to the front, knelt beside the freedman, and placed his hand on the man's. The pastor administered communion to them both, and the entire congregation rose and came forward together, black and white. They enjoyed the Lord's Supper together that day, and from that day on.[6]

General Lee would have had every excuse in the book if he had dressed down those soldiers, or left the church right then. But he turned a difficult situation into a learning and growing experience. Remember, circumstances do not dictate your character; they reveal it, and they become an opportunity to refine it.

When potential leaders learn that lesson, and live it, they are well on their way to being the kind of leaders that can turn a church around. And if God blesses you with leaders like that, your church will definitely be well on the way to being turned around! Godly character in leaders can overcome a host of weaknesses in ministry strategy and situation, but without it the best plans in the world will never succeed. That is why God summarizes all the qualifications for leadership by saying, "An overseer, then, must be above reproach" (1 Tim. 3:2). Leaders have to be respected for having true character.

This true character is a product of God's grace that is revealed by absolute dependence upon Christ, wholehearted devotion to Christ, and intentional discipline for Christ. True character develops from the inside out. It is a matter of the heart and soul. It doesn't happen overnight; it is developed over time. True character manifests self-denial, self-control, and self-development.

Content

What should be the *content*, or information, that our leaders in training need to learn? Obviously, they need to learn the doctrines of Scripture. A classic creed like the Westminster Confession of Faith would be helpful as a study tool, so that they are at least made aware of the biblical teaching on each important doctrine.

But let me suggest a few emphases that might otherwise be overlooked in a leadership training curriculum. First, it is important to spend some time helping trainees to understand history better (see chapter 2, pages 31–37, for a discussion of why this is important). Second, I would suggest that they learn to be proficient in the English Bible. Learning Greek and Hebrew would be wonderful if they have the opportunity, but most potential leaders do not. But they should know their way around the English Bible so that they can take people to Scripture when a question is asked about doctrine, and find key passages that relate to people's problems when they are involved in shepherding and counseling. There may have been a time in the past when potential leaders knew the Old Testament from the New, 1 Chronicles from 1 Corinthians, and the Gospels from the Epistles, but we cannot assume that anymore. Don't be surprised if your leader candidates need an elementary course in Bible introduction before they are ready to move on in their training.

Finally, make sure that they are well taught in one particular doctrine of Scripture. Understanding and applying the doctrine of *divine providence* will be absolutely essential for any church leaders, especially those in a church that needs revitalization. One reason is that an understanding of providence will help them to fight the temptation to despair, or give up, in the face of the challenges ahead.

Another great Civil War general, Stonewall Jackson, was shot by his own men at the height of his fame and success. He was thirty-nine years old and arguably the most famous man in the world, owing to his amazing victories in the early part of the war, which are studied and admired even today by military strategists. On the last day of Jackson's life, his doctor and his friends knew he was dying, but no one wanted to tell him. So the task fell to his wife, Mary Anna.

"Thomas," she asked him, "where would you want to be buried?"

"In Lexington," he said.

"What if I were to tell you that it is God's will for you to die today?"

"Mary Anna," Jackson replied, "if it is God's will for me to die today, then I prefer to die today. I will be an infinite gainer."

Jackson's wife finally broke down. She fell across his bed and began to weep uncontrollably. He put his hand on her and said, "Mary Anna, don't weep. Don't weep for me. Have you and I not always asked the Lord that we could meet Him on the Sabbath? And today is the Lord's Day. I shall see Him. Will you not rejoice with me that He in mercy has shown His providence to us?"

At 3:15 that afternoon of May 10, 1863, he took his last breath, trusting in God until the end.[7]

During the battle of Fredericksburg, Robert E. Lee received a note that his daughter Annie, who was preparing to be a missionary, had died. He could not go to her funeral because of the battle, so he wrote a letter to his eldest daughter:

> Mary, we cannot go to her, but she has gone to Him. Your mother cannot go because she is an invalid. Our friends will have to bury her. But will you not now join me in rejoicing before our God? For of my seven children He has taken the one that I know was ready to meet Him. Is

not God's providence good? In the midst of this evil He has mixed His mercy again. It now remains for us to bring this cruel war to a close. And our family circle to be unbroken there with Him.[8]

Not only does the doctrine of divine providence keep us out of the valley of despair during adversity, but it also keeps us from going off the scale in self-congratulation when God gives us victory. This is because we know that anything good comes from the hand of the Lord.

Another general from the Civil War provides us with an illustration of this truth, but this time it is a Union general. Joshua Chamberlain was a Bible teacher in Maine before the war started, and he was the only man who received a battlefield promotion from General Grant. He also was the man chosen to receive the surrender of the Confederate Army at Appomattox. And on that day in 1865 he did more than anyone else to promote healing between the North and the South.

When the remaining 8,900 soldiers of the Confederate Army surrendered, each brigade had to march to a place in front of the Union Army, and lay down their arms. As the first brigade approached, Joshua Chamberlain gave the command that the entire Union army should salute their defeated foes, with whom they had been locked in a deadly struggle for four years. And he repeated that salute for every Confederate brigade throughout the entire ceremony. Chamberlain said later that he thought he might be court-martialed for this gesture, but it aided the reunification of the country in untold ways. He was not court-martialed, but it probably did cost him a vice presidential nomination in 1868. He said it was worth it, though, because it was the right thing to do.[9]

Today, basketball players dunk over other players and then stare proudly at them as they are running back down the court. Baseball pitchers strike out batters and then fire an imaginary gun at them as they walk back to the dugout. But this Union general showed kindness and respect to those he had defeated—the same soldiers who had been killing people he loved during the war! This is because Joshua Chamberlain believed in the providence of God. He knew that his victory had only been achieved because it was permitted by a gracious God, not because he was better than anyone else.

When the fires of revitalization begin to burn in your church, and great things start happening, it is important that you and the other leaders know that it is not because you are so wonderful, or even that you are better than the previous leaders. A church goes from embers to a flame because God has mercy on it through the means He has ordained. To Him belongs all the glory.

Competency

What skills do potential leaders need to develop, as part of a training curriculum? It is not enough for them just to have character and knowledge; they also must have some experience and proven ability in the tasks that they will undertake as leaders. So I suggest a basic outline of three *m*'s, to help you remember the skills that leaders must develop.

Ministry skills. First, leaders must learn how to minister as a shepherd and overseer so that others may prosper and grow. In Acts 20:28, Paul told the Ephesian elders, "Be on guard for yourselves and for all the flock, among which the Holy Spirit has made you overseers, to shepherd the church of God which He purchased with His own blood." And Peter told another group of elders,

> I exhort the elders among you, as your fellow elder and witness of the sufferings of Christ, and a partaker also of the glory that is to be revealed, shepherd the flock of God among you, exercising oversight not under compulsion, but voluntarily, according to the will of God; and not for sordid gain, but with eagerness; nor yet as lording it over those allotted to your charge, but proving to be examples to the flock. And when the Chief Shepherd appears, you will receive the unfading crown of glory. (1 Peter 5:1–4)

Mentoring skills. Second, leaders in training must learn how to mentor, so that followers are taught the Word of God, and quality leadership is maintained and multiplied. Inherent in the role of a church leader is the requirement of reproducing yourself in other leaders. And those other leaders that you train must then reproduce themselves in others, and so on. This is the pattern that Paul laid down in 2 Timothy 2:2: "And the things which you have heard from me in the presence of many witnesses, these entrust to faithful men, who will be able to teach others also." So you should not simply be teaching men how to lead in the church, but should also be teaching them how to train other men to lead in the church.

Management skills. Third, you should train potential leaders to manage themselves, their families, and the church. In 1 Corinthians 9:27 the apostle Paul says, "I buffet my body and make it my slave, lest possibly, after I have preached to others, I myself should be disqualified." And 1 Timothy 3:4–5 says about an elder, "He must be one who manages his own household well, keeping his children under control with all dignity (but if a man does not know how to manage his own household, how will he take care of the church of God?)." Because management is an important part of the role of church leaders, those who are training for that position should be well aware of the policies and procedures of their particular church. And they should be given opportunities to manage prior to being put in that official position.

To help you as you seek to train people to be ministers, mentors, and managers, I have compiled a list of leadership principles and practices. Let me share with you a select few of them. The wisdom in them will help your current leaders, and your potential leaders, to become more competent for the glory of God.

- Effective leaders take risks, but don't deny reality.
- Effective leaders are innovative, but not ridiculous or novel just to gain attention.
- Effective leaders take charge, but do not oppress people.
- Effective leaders have high expectations that stretch others and raise the bar for all, but don't set people up for failure by demanding the impossible.
- Effective leaders maintain a positive attitude, but stay in touch with reality.
- Effective leaders create opportunities for success in small things that encourage others to tackle the greater challenges.
- Effective leaders lead from the front, but stay in touch with those who are following and supporting.
- Effective leaders give their people public credit for success, but take responsibility themselves for any failure or setback.

- Effective leaders plan their work and work their plan, and always remember that their plan and their work are people.
- Effective leaders establish priorities in their leadership plans, and stay with them.
- Effective leaders establish accountability for themselves and for their subordinates.
- Effective leaders raise the bar of performance for themselves.
- Effective leaders avoid bitterness and animosity toward those who are in opposition.
- Effective leaders avoid rationalizations and the public blaming of subordinates.
- Effective leaders clearly communicate their objectives and methods, as well as their expectations for others.
- Effective leaders ensure agreement and support by subordinates on vision, goals, philosophy, and tactics.
- Effective leaders are aware of their subordinates' preferences, strengths, and weaknesses.
- Effective leaders develop thoughtful loyalty from leader to follower, as well as from follower to leader.
- Effective leaders are courageous, yet avoid being foolhardy in the name of bravery.
- Effective leaders develop clear objectives and overall strategy, but maintain the ability to be flexible.

Hopefully, these thoughts, and the others we have discussed in this chapter, will help you to raise up godly leaders to share in the ministry of revitalizing your church. But in order to attract potential leaders, get them excited about the ministry, and *keep* them excited about the ministry, you need to understand and apply the principles of mission and vision. So read on to the next chapter.

1. What is the definition of a leader on page 119? Explain the meaning of each part of that definition.

2. Are you training other people to be leaders through education, embodiment, empowerment, and evaluation? Give specific examples.

3. How much ministry are you doing by yourself, and how much are you involving others, for the purpose of leadership development?

4. Review the examples of men with godly character mentioned in this chapter. What can we learn from each one?

5. How would you evaluate yourself and the other leaders in your church in light of the list of leadership principles and practices at the end of this chapter?

Mission and Vision

One day a man was walking in the country and saw a boy practicing archery against the side of a barn. The man was quite impressed with the boy's marksmanship when he saw that all his previous shots had been bull's-eyes! There were several targets painted on the barn, and each one had an arrow right in the center. So the man stopped to watch the boy's next shot. The boy pulled back his bow and let an arrow fly to a random spot on the side of the barn. Then he took a can of paint and drew a target around the arrow.

That is how many church leaders approach their ministries. They aim at nothing and then try to make it look like they know what they are doing! But in a church that needs revitalization, that approach will never work. There must be a clearly defined mission and vision, or the ministry will continue to flounder and decline. Jesus Himself understood His mission clearly, and He passed His vision on to other leaders who would help him carry it out. You must do the same if you want to be a successful shepherd like our Lord.

For the purposes of this chapter, I want to make a distinction between "mission" and "vision," though many people use the two terms with similar meanings. Your mission is what God has called your church *to do* for God's glory, whereas vision is what He wants your church *to be* as the mission is fulfilled. To put it another way, mission is our purpose, and vision is our passion.

This distinction is illustrated by the difference between Matthew 28:19–20 and Acts 1:8. In the first passage, Jesus tells His disciples what they will do ("Go therefore and make disciples of all nations"), and in the second He tells them what they will be ("You shall be My witnesses"). He gave them a purpose to fulfill, but He also told them what they would become as they fulfilled that mission.

A MISSION FROM GOD

The idea of mission is reflected in the description of David in Acts 13:36: "For David, after he had served the purpose of God in his own generation, fell asleep, and was laid among his fathers." David had a purpose for his existence, and that purpose was specific to *his own generation*. Likewise, God has raised up your church for a purpose, and that purpose is unique to the situation that God has put you in. So as you think about the mission of your church, you should think about your place in the world around you. It is not enough simply to say, "We exist to glorify God." That is a good start, but we must also think about *how* our church can glorify God, considering where we are and who we are.

What does it mean to be a downtown church? What does it mean to be a suburban church? What does it mean to be halfway between downtown and suburbia? Is there a particular need or dynamic that seems to characterize the area around the church? For instance, what would it mean to be a church in New England, in an area that has known the blessings of the Great Awakening, but has fallen under the onslaught of Unitarian universalism and is now steeped in pure secularism? On the other hand, how would the mission be different in part of the Bible Belt, or in a place like California, where there is very little Christian tradition upon which to draw?

This is an important consideration if we are to understand and articulate the purpose for our church and its ministries. Many pastors are planting and leading churches that would be wonderful if we were living in the 1750s. But we are not living in the 1750s. The message of the gospel and the ministry goals of the church are the same as always. But the way we communicate the gospel and the way we reach our ministry goals will have to change to fit the nature of the times. For instance, the technology of our age can be used for the propagation of the gospel, just as we praise the Lord for the use of the printing press during the Reformation. And while the answer the world always needs to hear is the gospel of grace in Christ, the questions that are asked by the world change from generation to generation and from culture to culture. If we love people, we will not only speak the truth, but also listen to them in love and try to understand their perspective.

In the 1970s, I became a Christian while attending East Carolina University. There were times during my classes when Christianity was attacked, such as when my history professor threw the Bible across the room. I was desperately trying to defend my faith against these attacks, and I would have given anything for Josh McDowell to ride over the hill on his white horse to tell them all why Christianity was the most reasonable system of truth. The debate when I was in college was whether Christianity was true or not. But that is not the debate that today's college student will be engaging in. The question today is, Is there any truth at all? We live in an age of skepticism and relativism.

And how do we enter into that debate? That is the kind of question we need to ask ourselves when we consider the mission of our church. The apostle Paul recognized the importance of context in his ministry, of course. We learn in the book of Acts that when he went to the Jewish synagogue, he preached Jesus from the Old Testament. But when he went to the Greek marketplace in Athens, he started with the existence of God and the fact of creation (Acts 17:22–25). He knew that the Jews already believed in God and His written revelation, and he knew that the Greeks did not. So even though his message and goals were the same, he tailored his ministry to the situation he was in.

STATE YOUR MISSION

An important step in developing the mission of your church is to create or refine a mission statement. When I became the new pastor of Briarwood Presbyterian Church in 1999, I requested that we keep the same mission statement that the church already had. This was a good way of connecting to the past, rather than changing everything right away, and I also thought that the statement was a very good one. Here it is:

For God's glory Briarwood desires to equip Christians to worship God and to reach Birmingham to reach the world for Christ.

That is a good mission statement, first of all, because it is based entirely on Scripture. It mentions God's glory as the purpose for all we do (1 Cor. 10:31), it says that we are primarily to be equipping Christians (Eph. 4:11–12), it emphasizes the importance of worship (John 4:23–24), and it includes the worldwide scope of the Great Commission (Matt. 28:19–20; Acts 1:8). But another reason why it is such a good statement is that it answers the questions that any such statement should answer. And as you consider the mission of your church, your statement should also answer these five questions: Who are we? What do we do? Where do we do this? How do we do this? Why do we do this?[1]

Who are we? Your mission statement should include a reference to who you are, because your mission requires a clear understanding of that. In the case of our church, we are Briarwood Presbyterian Church. We are not First Baptist Church, St. John's Catholic Church, or the Adventure Church. And we are a *church,* not a political organization, a social club, or a sports team. This should all be obvious, of course, but it gives me an opportunity to make the point that understanding and articulating who we are is foundational to understanding and articulating the mission we have been called to.

What do we do? At Briarwood, we focus on *worshiping* God and *reaching* people for Christ. Our priorities are made clear in the statement, and it also implies an order within those priorities, where edification logically comes before evangelism

149

(see below). So the statement can help us communicate to new people what they can expect from the church, and it can also help us in evaluating issues that we face as leaders. For instance, when someone in the body proposes a new ministry, we can ask, Will this ministry help people to worship God and reach others for Christ? In this way, our mission statement helps us to use our energies and resources more wisely, and to avoid rabbit trails that might be a waste of time.

Where do we do this? We originate our ministry in Birmingham, but we consciously do it in Birmingham in order to minister to the world. So there should be no surprise when a mission conference shows up on the church schedule. There should be no surprise when we ask people each year to give to overseas ministries. There should be no surprise when people are asked to show hospitality to missionaries and their families, because that is part of our mission. Our mission extends beyond Birmingham to the whole world. But it does start in our home city, and so we are not going to do something out there without committing to do it ourselves right here. We want to send out there what we are doing right here.

How do we do this? We do this by *equipping* Christians. This sets Briarwood apart from some other churches. We are not a church that is primarily for "seekers." We are an equipping church that trains people to seek and save the lost. So when we assemble in our worship services, classes, and small groups, we intentionally focus on equipping Christians. We do try the best we can to be sensitive to nonbelievers and to address their needs as well. But our primary purpose is clearly to equip Christians, because we believe that the church has a significant impact on the world, not when we rely on people coming to our buildings to find Christ, but when we take Christ to them where they are in the world. We hope that our people, when they are built up in the faith, will be like the early believers in Acts 8:4, which says that "those who had been scattered went about preaching the word."[2]

Why do we do this? We do this for God's glory. We do this so that God will be satisfied and gratified. By beginning our mission statement with this phrase, we remind ourselves, and anyone else who reads it, that we exist for God's glory rather than for our own. And this is a necessary reminder because we so often can forget who is the most important Person in the church. As the great English preacher Charles Spurgeon once said,

> "To whom be glory forever" (2 Tim. 4:18). This should be the single desire of the Christian. I take it that he should not have twenty wishes, but only one. He may desire to see his family brought up well, but only that "to God may be glory forever." He may wish for prosperity in business, but only so far as it may help him to promote this: "to whom be glory forever." He may desire to attain more gifts and more graces, but it should only be that "to him may be glory forever." This one thing I know, Christian: You are not acting as you ought to do when you are moved by any other motive than the one motive of your Lord's glory.[3]

And a church is not acting as it ought to unless it is committed to God's glory above all. As Paul said in 2 Corinthians 5:9, we must "have as our ambition, whether at home or absent, *to be pleasing to Him.*"

DEVELOPING A VISION

If mission is God's purpose for your church in your own generation, then vision is the ability to picture that purpose implemented in your world. Vision must start with the mission statement, because you have to know first what God is calling you to do. But then you need to move on to ask, What will this look like in our situation? What do we want our church to be, if the Lord wills? What are our hopes and dreams for the next five years, the next ten years, the next twenty years, the next generation?

In order to develop such a vision, the leaders of the church should consider the following issues.

The pastor's strengths, weaknesses, and calling. First, a vision for the church must take into account the pastor's passion and giftedness. I believe that churches should have a plurality of elders, that leadership should be shared, and that the vision must be owned and implemented by more than one man. But though I have never seen a church move forward without a plurality of leaders, I also have never seen a group of leaders move forward without one man who is clearly the leader among them. This kind of leader does not demand authority or influence over the others, nor does he intentionally place himself in a position above them. But by virtue of the skills he has and the respect accorded to him, he takes a primary role in setting the vision for the church. And I believe that that man should be the pastor.

Having said that, however, I want to make it clear that a church will never go from embers to a flame unless the pastor's vision is given away and is embraced, enhanced, and enlarged by the other leaders. If the vision belongs only to the pastor, and not to the other leaders, it will never get to the congregation. And if the congregation has no sense of ownership in the vision, it will die stillborn. How many people who rent a car will wash it before they return it to the agency? Very few, if any, because they do not own the car. So they are unconcerned about maintaining it or improving it. The same is true in a church; if the people do not take ownership of the ministry, they will assume it belongs to the pastor and leave him to take care of it. So, pastor, don't set yourself up as the proprietor of the church! Develop a vision, but make it a priority to share it with the people who can really make it happen.

Because the vision usually starts with the pastor, however, and because he will remain a key person in its implementation, his passion and giftedness must be carefully considered. The pastor himself, and the other leaders who serve with him, should ask questions like these: Why are you here at this church? Why do you believe God called you here? What is God's purpose for you and for this congregation as the pastor of this church, responsible for the ministry of the Word and the sacraments?

What are the pastors strengths and weaknesses? The other leaders should not focus primarily on the pastor's weaknesses; rather, they should play to his strengths. He should address his weaknesses, and receive regular assessments of how he is progressing in those areas. But the other leaders should be excited about his strengths and make the most of them. If I were a baseball coach, I would not have our power hitter lead off just because someone said, "He should be hitting more singles." No, his strength is hitting the ball where you don't find it anymore. So I would have him bat fourth, so that there would usually be somebody on base when he came to the plate. I'd want to play to his strengths. I would also tell him that he should learn to hit to the opposite field and get a single every once in a while, so that other teams would have to pitch honestly to him. I would want him to work on his weaknesses, but we would still play to his strengths. So it should be with a pastor. Find out what his strengths are and make the most of them.

The congregation's opportunities. A vision for the church should also take into account the congregation's location, opportunities, assets, and resources. Think about where you are in your world and what you have to offer. At Briarwood, for instance, we have many businesspeople who have connections throughout the world. We would be foolish if we did not use this resource to support missions. We also receive more income through giving than many other churches, so naturally we can help other churches get started. We are located in Birmingham, Alabama—not in Boaz, Alabama. We will do some things that a church in Boaz will also be doing, of course. But we should also be doing some things that a church in Boaz *cannot* do. For example, since we are in Birmingham, should not one of our goals be to present to the world the power of the gospel in racial reconciliation among God's people?

So, when you think about a vision for your church, ask questions like these: Where is our church located? What are our assets and resources? And how can God use these things to advance His kingdom?

The ministries of other local churches. Next, you should consider the location and ministries of other churches in the area. What are the churches around you doing, and how can your ministry be unique among them? When I was the pastor at Christ Covenant Church in Charlotte, we were praying and talking about a vision for our music ministry. Someone suggested that we do concerts, but I was concerned that concerts tend to be more conducive to Christian entertainment than to worship or evangelism. (I don't think there is anything necessarily wrong with Christian entertainment, but it did not fit very well with our mission statement.) I also mentioned that down the road from us was a church that presented twenty-one concerts per year, with big names and high-quality production. We were talking about trying to duplicate what they did so well, and so I suggested that we come up with something different, something that would fit in better with our mission.

So our music people ran with that vision and developed a Christian jazz band that appealed more to unchurched people than the churched people who were attending the other local concerts. They began to do outdoor concerts on Saturday. We had people coming to listen to that band who would never go to a Christian concert, and who would never have come to church on Sunday morning. But during the concert, the musicians would share their testimonies or tell the audience that they wanted their pastor to explain some things about why they play their music. The jazz band got them in the back door, and I got a chance to tell them about Christ.

We did not need to repeat what was going on a few miles down the road. If our people wanted such concerts, they could go and enjoy them. Instead, we took our resources and used them for something unique, to meet a need that was not being met elsewhere. In the same way, you should be aware of what is already happening in your community and see if you can develop ministries that will contribute something new.

The needs of the community. Finally, a vision for your church should be based on the needs and opportunities in the community. The leaders of your church should be students of the culture around them, being aware of the unique dynamics that characterize the particular area where the church is located. What kinds of people live in the area? What is their background? What do they believe, and what is important to them? What has happened in the past in that community that everyone would know about? Have there been changes there in recent history?

When I went to Miami in 1980 to become the pastor of Pinelands Presbyterian Church, I discovered that the community had changed drastically since the church was started in 1959. Back at that time, many people were moving south to Florida, to live in retirement. Many of them could not afford to live in Fort Lauderdale and the area known as "the Gold Coast," but it was not as expensive south of Miami. So middle-class families were moving to that area by the droves. And as they were beginning their new lives in Florida, they would need to find new stores to shop in, new schools for their children to attend, new doctors to care for them—and many would be looking for a new church to join. Some of them, in fact, were looking for a Presbyterian church. So the original pastor of Pinelands in 1959 planted a pretty good Presbyterian church that would meet the needs of those new people. The church was what some have called a "receptor church." It grew to nine hundred people attending, largely by *receiving* those who were moving into the area and looking for a good Presbyterian church.

But when I got there in 1980, the community had become multicultural. Apart from a couple from Texas and a man from Nebraska (who turned out to be the local drug dealer), the neighbors on my street were a Jewish couple from New York, a couple from the Dominican Republic, another from Jamaica, and another from Granada. The good news was that the people from the West Indies spoke English; the bad news was that none of them had moved into town looking for a Presbyterian church!

So we had to change our mind-set from that of a "receptor" church to that of a "mission" church. Fortunately, the mission field had come to us, but we still had to find ways to connect with the different cultures that God had called us to reach. Some people suggest that when a community changes drastically around a church, it is time to sell the building and move out to another area that has the kind of people that used to be in the church. I do not agree, in most cases. I think that if God has provided a building there, an adjustment ought to be made in the ministry before the church gives up on that area. Or, if another church needs to be planted elsewhere, the ministry should continue at the existing church under leaders who are better gifted to reach that area.

Sometimes the community changes in other ways, too. I became a Christian many years ago in a church in Charlotte, North Carolina, that today has only about a dozen people in it. At one time, if you wanted a church that was evangelical, Reformed, and Presbyterian, that church was the only option. So they had hundreds of people attending. But today, with the growth of the Presbyterian Church in America and the rebirth of the Associate Reformed Presbyterian Church in the area, there are literally scores of options for people who want that kind of church. I sat down with the leadership and said, "You should throw a victory party, because what you have stood for has been multiplied all over this city. But you now have to realize that you can't just set up shop and expect people to travel from far away to your church. You now have to look at the people living within three to five miles of this church building.

157

Who is living here, and how are you going to reach them? Unless you have a phenomenal pulpiteer, people are not going to drive by five similar churches to come here. You need to realize that something has changed around you and make some adjustments."

Likewise, you need to look at the situation around you—not the situation as it used to be, but as it is right now. Neighborhoods change. Who lives there now? Whom do you need to reach? What are their special needs? As you study the dynamics of the community around you and factor them into your vision, you will gain the wisdom you need to see your church go from embers to a flame.

VISION AT WORK

The vision of Briarwood Presbyterian is that we desire to be an "epicenter church." An epicenter is where an earthquake starts. It sends out shock waves through the ground for miles in every direction. It sends out tidal waves through the sea. We are asking God to cause a "gospel earthquake" at our church, which will then radiate in every direction so that we will be an epicenter of revival in our time. The kind of tremors we want to see are evangelism, discipleship, church planting, church revitalization, and deeds of love, mercy, and justice.

This is the kind of ministry that took place in the early church, of course. And this is how the gospel spread throughout the whole world. Paul planted churches through biblical evangelism and discipleship. Then he worked at revitalizing and strengthening the churches he had planted. He committed himself to deeds of love, mercy, and justice, and he taught those churches how to carry out that kind of ministry. Several of those churches became epicenters of gospel ministry, sending out missionaries and planting more churches in their surrounding areas.

The goal of the leaders at Briarwood is that our church would be that kind of body. We want to get people excited about being part of a church like that and about the impact we will have on the world through our ministries. It is important to communicate this vision because there is no greater way to provide motivation for the members and potential members of a church. Nothing motivates people more for creative, sacrificial, joyful, and continual support of a ministry than vision. It is certainly a more powerful motivation than guilt, which is the lever church leaders use more than any other. They tell the congregation, for instance, "We need nursery workers. How can you sit in this church week after week while other people are caring for your children, and never take a turn in the nursery yourself?" Instead of helping people find their passion and then use their gifts, they crack the whip to get them into line.

How many people do you think are consistently motivated by such an approach? I would suggest that there are only a few, and most of them are the kind of people who are probably motivated too much by guilt. We should be giving such people better motives—gospel motives—for their ministry. I also would suggest that guilt may motivate people once, or maybe twice, but it cannot provide incentive for creative, sacrificial, joyful, and continual service. And it is not conducive to spiritual growth, either, as Bryan Chappell explains:

> If we serve God because we believe he will love us less if we do not, punish us more if we do less, or bless us more if we do more, then we are not worshipping God with our actions; we are only pursuing our self-interests. In this case the goal of our lives is personal promotion or

personal protection rather than the glory of God, and even our seemingly moral activities are a transgression of the first commandment. Grace does not change the rules Scripture truly requires; rather it makes adherence to them true obedience.

Guilt drives the unrepentant to the cross, but grace must lead believers from there or we cannot serve God.[4]

When an exciting vision is presented, and people are motivated by the grace of God toward them, they are moved by the Holy Spirit to participate in God's work.

Greeting people after my message one Sunday, I met a man and a woman who were visiting the church for the first time. The woman was half the man's age, but I'm glad I did not ask, "Is this your daughter?" because it turned out to be his third wife. He was a highly successful businessman, who had been a decorated "top gun" pilot in the Navy for many years. (He had even flown in the Blue Angels at one time.) They were touched by the message and had questions about spiritual issues, so I set up an appointment and met with both of them. By God's grace, the husband became a Christian, and the wife rededicated her life to Christ after years of wandering from Him. They both started attending our church regularly.

A few weeks later we had a missions trip scheduled to Jamaica with a ministry called JAARS (Jungle Aviation and Radio Service). I encouraged the man to join the trip, and he agreed. The team flew off to Jamaica in a fifty-year-old DC-3 owned by the missionary organization. As I saw them off, I felt like I should lay hands on that old plane and pray that it would make it both ways. My new brother must have been quite unimpressed by the plane also, because when he came back, he had a proposition for me. He told me that he had just closed a big real estate deal in which part of his commission was a new twin-engine Aztec plane.

"I already own one plane, and I really don't need two," he told me. "So I have this idea. How about if I let JAARS use the new plane whenever they need it? I'll maintain it and keep it in my name, and then if you ever need a ride to a speaking engagement, I'll fly you there."

I had no idea when I woke up that morning that I was going to have my own plane and my own pilot! Nor did JAARS ever expect to have a new Aztec at their disposal. But it happened because of the power of the gospel and the power of vision. He had seen the need in Jamaica, and he had seen the steps JAARS was taking to reach it for Christ. The resources that this man had were mobilized for ministry, because he saw something worth giving to. No one motivated him to do this out of guilt; in fact, no one even asked him to do this. He voluntarily gave of himself and his resources when his heart was gripped by Christ, and when he was exposed to a ministry that was exalting and honoring Christ.

This illustrates an important truth about church ministry, one that relates especially to churches in need of revitalization. Leaders in such churches often think that they do not have enough resources to "think big" or to develop a vision that involves doing great things for God. But I have observed over the years that resources seldom precede vision and ministry. On the contrary, when a vision is articulated and ministry is begun in the direction of that vision, other leaders are drawn to the cause and resources begin to pour in. So instead of asking, How can we get more resources so that we can develop some goals? I would suggest that you develop your mission and vision, and begin to implement it. As it affects people, they will creatively, sacrificially, and joyfully supply the needed resources. You may find that there are resources in your church and your community that will remain untapped until you develop and pursue a vision that honors the Lord.

Resources seldom precede ministry. They follow it, affirm it, and expand it. Resources follow effective ministry, and that kind of ministry occurs when competent leaders cluster around the biblical vision of a godly visionary.

FARSIGHTED VISION

A vision that will honor the Lord and excite people about your church cannot be limited to immediate and short-term goals. Such goals are important, to mark progress and provide small victories along the way, but your vision should extend well beyond the near future. You should be able to answer the question, How will what we do today benefit the next generation, and the next, and ten generations after that, if the Lord tarries?

I read about a great example of this recently. There is a college at Oxford that has a beautiful, four-hundred-year-old chapel, featuring an expansive oak-beamed ceiling. Some time ago they had the roof examined, and the inspectors informed them that if the oak worms quit holding hands, they were in big trouble. The ceiling was about to collapse, and they would need a new one.

The college knew that they could not possibly afford to import enough oak to duplicate the existing beams, so they proceeded to plan B and then plan C, trying to figure out something that would work on this wonderful, historic building. But as they were in the process, someone did some research and found out that four hundred years ago, the builders of the chapel knew about oak worms, and so they had bought three acres of land at another location and planted oak trees on it!

All the college had to do was harvest the oak trees and then rebuild the ceiling, thanks to the foresight of their forefathers!

Now that is vision. Most of us only plan for the moment, or maybe the near future. We have a plastic, throwaway society. Those people, however, built something of substance and reasoned, *If Jesus tarries, we want to take care of those who will come twelve generations later.* That is vision, and that kind of long-term vision motivates people and draws resources into action.

At Briarwood, we have attempted to incorporate the principles I have been discussing into a statement of vision called "The 100 Plan." The vision of your church will look much different than ours, of course, but I want to share ours with you so that you can see an example of the kind of thinking I have been encouraging you to do. Here are the goals we have for the next ten years at our church, the effects of which will reach far into the future, God willing:

1. To initiate an average of 100 small-group ministries each year devoted to implement W.E.L.L., the Briarwood discipleship "fitness plan."[5]
2. To average 100 professions of faith each quarter of every year through the Briarwood evangelistic ministries, while seeking to average 100 professions of faith each year from Briarwood new members, and also graduating 100 Briarwood members annually through E.E.
3. To plant a strategic "network" of 100 epicenter churches throughout North America and the world which are intentionally committed to a biblical ministry model.
4. To systematically shepherd 100 churches in North America through the Briarwood revitalization ministry "From Embers to a Flame."

5. To mentor 100 interns through the Briarwood ministry model and place them in strategic ministries of gospel church planting or revitalization.

6. To shepherd 100 strategic cross-cultural churches through the Briarwood revitalization ministry "From Embers to a Flame."

7. To place 100 cross-cultural missionaries for church planting or revitalization in strategic epicenters throughout the world and support them with 100 short-term mission trips.

8. To implement 100 urban/ethnic ministry initiatives, church plants, or revitalization projects developed through a selected and qualified strategic planning team.

9. To graduate 100 African-American seminarians.

10. To invest 100 million dollars in the Briarwood mercy, benevolence, evangelistic, and mission initiatives to achieve "The 100 Plan: A Bridge to the 21st Century."

These goals may seem out of reach, even for a larger church, but I sincerely believe that God can accomplish them, if they are consistent with His sovereign and revealed will. God is pleased with such desires of the heart because they express a faith in His power and an utter dependence on His grace.

A friend of mine, Randy Pope, is the senior pastor of Perimeter Church in the Atlanta area. He challenged me over twenty years ago with his visionary leadership. Perimeter Church adopted this motto:

> We want to attempt something so great for God that it is doomed to failure unless God is in it.

Likewise, if you want to see revitalization in your church, you need to have a God-sized vision, not a man-sized vision. Then, when the Lord accomplishes His work through you, others will only be able to say: "This is the Lord's doing. Great things He has done. Praise His name forever."

QUESTIONS

1. Does your church have a mission statement? If so, does it answer the five questions on pages 149–51?

2. Does your church leadership have a vision for ministry that is known well enough by the members that they could share it with others?

3. How would you evaluate your church's current mission and vision in light of this chapter? Put something down on paper if you have not already done so.

Great Commission Discipleship

No Bible passage should inform our mission, and shape our vision, more than the Great Commission in Matthew 28:16–20:

> The eleven disciples proceeded to Galilee, to the mountain which Jesus had designated. And when they saw Him, they worshiped Him; but some were doubtful. And Jesus came up and spoke to them, saying, "All authority has been given to Me in heaven and on earth. Go therefore and make disciples of all the nations, baptizing them in the name of the Father and the Son and the Holy Spirit, teaching them to observe all that I commanded you; and lo, I am with you always, even to the end of the age."

As you think through your church's mission and vision, and as you proceed to recover all the "first things" that will bring revitalization, this passage provides a helpful overview of the dynamics that God will use to take you from embers to a flame. A discussion of the Great Commission is fitting for the last chapter of this book, because it tells us what will be happening in a church when it is renewed by God's power, and provides a standard for the evaluation of our progress along the way.

THE DYNAMIC OF "UPREACH" (AUTHENTIC WORSHIP)

The role of worship in the Great Commission is often overlooked, but the disciples were worshiping when Jesus spoke His famous words to them. Matthew 28:16–17 says, "The eleven disciples proceeded to Galilee, to the mountain which Jesus had designated. And when they saw Him, they worshiped Him." So the narrative illustrates that corporate worship provides a necessary foundation upon which the rest of the Great Commission is built. And if your church is to be revitalized by the Spirit of God, you must first be worshiping Him in spirit and in truth (John 4:24).

As a way of helping you to think through the kind of worship that should be happening in your church, we will discuss some contemporary models that present goals that are valid consequences of worship, but invalid objectives of worship. God's people usually do not worship in ways that are directly contrary to Scripture, but we do often focus on one aspect to the exclusion of others. We also often fail to keep the exaltation of Christ as the primary purpose of our worship.

The entertainment model. In this approach to corporate worship, the plans for the Sunday service are controlled by questions like Is everybody having a good time? The primary concern is whether people are enjoying themselves when they come to church. Above all, we want them to have a pleasant experience so that they will want to come back. So we provide entertainment for them, because that is what modern people like.

There are many problems with this approach, of course, not the least of which is that God's people are to be participants, not spectators, in worship. Also, some elements of biblical corporate worship will never fit into an entertainment model, such as reflection, meditation, confession of sin, and intercessory prayer.

The edification model. In this model, worship is focused on how much the believers will get out of it. If someone misses Sunday worship, for instance, the main concern is with the blessings that they have not received. People who miss a service are gently chided by the admonishment, "You should have been here because you sure missed a blessing." There is very little thought about blessing God, because the focus is on what the worship is supposed to do for people. One writer explains the symptoms of this approach well:

> Individualistic self-indulgence is displayed often by disgruntled parishioners who believe that they are not being "fed" in worship. Worship exists, they argue, "to feed me"—meaning "to please me." The pleasure they get out of worship becomes the test of its validity. However, the worshiper who is always calculating what he or she is "getting out" of the service is missing the essence of worship: worship is not introverted. It is extroverted—we give to God as we celebrate his acts. That is the essence of worship. When personal gratification is worship's objective, worship is invalidated. To leave the service with

the query, "Now what did I get out of church today?" is to misunderstand the nature of worship.[1]

The evangelism model. For some, the main purpose of the "worship service" is to reach unbelievers for Christ. I put "worship service" in quotes because when that goal is foremost, the weekly meeting is actually mislabeled. It is more like an outreach event than a worship service. In fact, many call it a "seeker-centered worship service." That seems to be an oxymoron. How can it be a *worship* service if it is seeker-centered instead of God-centered?

In 1 Corinthians 14:23–25, Paul implies that the church is to gather primarily for worship, and our focus on God will actually draw unbelievers to Christ. This has been called "doxological evangelism":

> If therefore the whole church should assemble together and all speak in tongues, and ungifted men or unbelievers enter, will they not say that you are mad? But if all prophesy, and an unbeliever or an ungifted man enters, he is convicted by all, he is called to account by all; the secrets of his heart are disclosed; and so he will fall on his face and worship God, declaring that God is certainly among you.

So it would seem that the first purpose of corporate worship is the exaltation of God, that the second purpose is the edification of believers, and that evangelism is a consequence when unbelievers can see that God is in our midst.

The executive model. Some church leaders view worship primarily as a way to accomplish the goals they have set for the church, or to get something done that needs to be done. In this

170

model the worship service becomes a gathering of stockholders, with the pastor as chairman of the board, there to inspire everyone, and the elders as the board of directors. Beware of such a pragmatic or mechanistic approach to worship, because it will take the focus off the One for whom we gather. The worship in your church should certainly fit with your mission and vision, but the glory of God must remain your primary purpose.

The education model. This is a common error, especially among churches that love the Word of God. Worship is viewed as primarily for the purpose of teaching, with the sermon as the only part that is truly important. This approach was exemplified by a man I once knew who arrived late to church every week, right at the beginning of the message. When I asked him why, he said, "I am just skipping the preliminaries." By that he meant the other elements of the worship service, such as the singing, prayers, and offering. So I told him to go ask Ananias and Sapphira if the offering was just a preliminary (Acts 5:1–11)!

Another pastor once told me that his church did not take up an offering in their worship service, because they wanted people to know that they were not there for their money. I think that reveals a misunderstanding of the purpose for the offering. The main purpose for the offering is not for the church to get money from the people, but for the people to worship God with His tithe and their offerings. And it is the same for the psalms, hymns, and spiritual songs—they are not just a good idea or a "warm up" for the message, although they can help us to focus and prepare our hearts for the preaching of the Word. The singing itself is worship of God. Likewise, the confession of sin is worship. The reciting of creeds is worship. The Bible reading and the sacraments are worship. And even the preaching itself

171

should be considered part of worship, not merely an opportunity to learn something (see chapter 5, page 110).

People should enjoy worshiping God. They should be edified and blessed. People should be won to Christ in our worship services. The church does get its marching orders in the context of worship. And people should learn something in worship. But these are *consequences* of true worship, rather than the *essence or objective* of true worship.

What is the essence and objective of worship? It is this: "Rejoice *in the Lord*." What brings joy to the heart, the unbeliever to Christ, blessing to the believer, instruction in the Christian life, and direction for God's people? It is the exaltation of God in the supremacy and sufficiency of Christ as Creator, Redeemer, and Sustainer for the glory of the Father. What is happening in true worship? "Bless the Lord, O my soul." What happens to me when I bless the Lord? I get blessed. When I "worship the Lord and serve Him only," I am served and edified by God Himself.

When God is at the center of our worship, and His Word is being preached to His people, unbelievers will also be moved to glorify Him. And the church will get its marching orders. And the people will learn the Word of God. But again, those are all consequences of true worship, not its essence. If we make any of those things the center of our worship, we not only fail to worship, but are participating in idolatry, like the people of Israel did so often. And like those ancient people, when we have been idolatrous and have prostituted worship for a man-centered purpose instead of the glory of God, we will find ourselves in the place of judgment (1 Cor. 10:1–12).

The Greek word for worship is *latreia,* and the word for false worship is *eidōlolatreia* ("idolatry"). The worship in your church will be one or the other—there are no other options.

You need to understand what kind of worship is acceptable to God, and what kind is not, and teach that to your people. The Lord will not revitalize a church that is not worshiping Him in spirit and in truth.

The Dynamic of "OutReach" (Evangelism)

In Matthew 28:18–19, Jesus says, "Go therefore and make disciples," and the Greek text literally reads, "As you are going, make disciples." The participial form of the verb "go" assumes that believers will be going out into the world, and the point is that while we are going, we should be making disciples. Does this lessen the force of the command to go, as some have implied? On the contrary, in a way this *strengthens* the call for intentional evangelism, because it indicates that all true believers will be seeking for the lost as an inevitable fruit of being born again. Jesus assumes that His people will be reaching out to non-Christians, and He then proceeds to tell them how they should go about it.[2]

The church should be "going." We are not waiting for the seekers to come—we are going, like Jesus, "to seek and save the lost." Jesus came into the world seeking us; we are going into the world seeking them. And the Scriptures tell us much about what this evangelism should look like.

Intentional evangelism. Our evangelism should be intentional. We cannot just sit back and wait for unbelievers to come to us or to begin conversations with us about spiritual issues. And I would suggest that the longer someone has been a Christian, the more intentional evangelism should be, because it does not come as naturally to older believers as it does to new believers. Have you noticed that new Christians lead the most people to Christ? That is because they are still so amazed at the grace of God, and because they have so many friends and acquaintances who are unbelievers.

I remember when I first became a Christian, I had a long-time friend named Larry. I wondered how I was going to tell him about my new faith, and the Lord answered my prayer one day when my wife and I ran into him in a convenience store parking lot. While we were sitting in the car, I had my door open and Larry noticed a Bible in my car and asked me about it. I said that I had become a Christian, and started spilling the whole long story to him while we continued sitting in our cars. The more I talked, however, the more his car began to roll forward, and pretty soon he was gone! I remember thinking that there was no way Larry would ever become a Christian, because my evangelistic technique had been so pathetic. I turned to my wife and asked how she thought it had gone. Her answer was, "Not too well."

Two weeks later, however, a lady ran up to me in a restaurant and threw her arms around me, saying, "Harry Reeder, I just love you!" I had recently married Cindy and was suddenly wondering if this lady was "a blast from the past"! I turned around, and to my relief it was Larry's mother. She told me that Larry had just become a Christian. He had gone to church that week and committed his life to Christ. I asked her if it had anything to do with what I had said to him in the car two weeks before. She replied, "No, what you said didn't make a whole lot of sense to him. But he figured that if it could change somebody like you that much, he wanted to go check on it."

The testimony of new believers has that kind of power because of the transformation of their lives that is taking place right in front of their friends and family. But after we have been Christians for a while, we have to work harder to find ways to share the gospel with others. After being Christians for a while, we can become "used to" the gospel, instead of amazed by it, and most of our friends are now Christians. The answer? Stay amazed by the gospel. And intentionally seek relationships with the lost so that you can share the gospel with them.

Ongoing evangelism. Remember also that evangelism is a process. Conversion is an event that happens at one time, but the steps leading up to it often take a long time. Encourage the people in your church by reminding them that sometimes we are planting, and sometimes we are watering, and sometimes we are cultivating, and sometimes we are reaping. It is always a process. I have never yet led anyone to Christ when it was the first time anyone had talked to him or her about Jesus. In every case, somebody had already talked to them. Somebody had prayed for them. The seeds had already been planted.

Confrontational evangelism. Evangelism must be confrontational. It is good to build relationships with nonbelieving people, as many have pointed out, but somewhere along the line they need to be told that they are sinners who will end up in hell unless they come to Jesus. We should communicate these truths in the best way we can, of course, with love and courtesy and as much tact as the subject allows (Eph. 4:15; Col. 4:6). But we have to tell them the truth, and sooner or later that gets confrontational.

I am concerned that sometimes when Christians talk about "friendship evangelism," they mean making friends with people without ever telling them about the gospel. We have to remember that "faith comes from hearing, and hearing by the word of Christ" (Rom. 10:17). People will never come to Christ

175

unless they hear the message. So befriend others, by all means. Treat people with dignity. Treat people with respect. Listen to them. Talk with them about what interests them. Develop the relationship. But share the gospel. And remember that the point of evangelism is not to make a friend. The point is to help people make friends with Jesus.

Creative evangelism. Evangelism should also be thoughtful and creative. It is an exciting challenge, and it is so rewarding when we find ways to connect with non-Christians. For instance, I like to use my love for golf as a conduit for evangelism. Once I was out playing golf, and I asked one of the unbelievers I was playing with what he did for a job. He answered me, and then asked, "What about yours?" So I proceeded to tell him, "I have a great job. My boss hires people all the time, and he never fires anyone once he has hired them. I have total job security, and the benefits are out of this world." The man looked at me funny for a while, and then said, "What are you, a preacher?" So I didn't stump him like I had hoped, but I did get to tell him about Christ!

One of the reasons I have studied the lives of Christian men like Robert E. Lee, George Washington Carver, Teddy Roosevelt, Booker T. Washington, and Stonewall Jackson is that it enables me to connect with people in the world and share the gospel with them. I get invitations to speak about those men regularly. For instance, I was once invited to speak to a genealogical society about Lee's family tree. Most of the people there were Mormons. In the question-and-answer session, someone asked about Lee's "spiritual life," and I was able to explain his commitment to Christ and the impact it had on his life.

Any Christian can find something to have in common with unbelievers or of interest to them. If you don't already have something like that, you could take about twenty minutes a day to become an expert on something that will open up doors for evangelism. It could be gardening, tennis, movies, or many other things. But find creative ways to communicate the gospel.

Dialogical evangelism. Evangelism should be a dialogue. The best personal communication is two-way, so learn to ask people questions. You can find out where people are spiritually, and challenge them to think about their faith, through questions like the ones suggested by Evangelism Explosion. You can ask them, "If you were to die tonight, do you know where you would be?" And if they answer "Heaven," ask them why. Another good one is, "If you were to die tonight and stand before God, and He were to ask you, 'Why should I let you into My heaven?'—what would you say?" Both of those questions get to the heart of the issue you want to discuss with them: On what basis can we have a relationship with God? Making use of a program like EE would help the people in your church to get over their fears of evangelizing, and equip them with some basic tools to use as they are "going."

Multifaceted evangelism. Finally, evangelism in the church needs to be multifaceted, not just one program. As good as EE is, you need to have other forms of outreach as well. Some possibilities are special events, mercy ministries that include a way of sharing the gospel, planning for non-Christians who will attend on Christmas and Easter, and music ministries like the jazz band I mentioned before. The more you diversify your investments in evangelism, the more profitable they will prove to be.

THE DYNAMIC OF INREACH (ENFOLDING)

The Great Commission says that we are to "make disciples . . . *baptizing them* in the name of the Father and the Son and the Holy Spirit." This speaks of the need not only to reach out to people outside the church with the gospel, but also to *pull them in* to the family of the church. This process can be called enfolding or assimilation, and it is an essential aspect of church revitalization. You could attract all kinds of attention through wonderful services and tremendous outreach ministries, but if the people you reach are not brought into the body, the church will continue to die. And I would suggest that relationships are the key to assimilation. Discipleship must be relational, not only informational.

From personal observation, I have become convinced that there are three keys to assimilation or enfolding new believers and members into a local church. First, they must be hearing something from God's Word that is challenging and changing their lives from the teaching ministries of the church. Second, they must have a place and ministry in the church that matches their personal calling and passion. Every ministry in the church should have some low-level entry points into their ministry where new members can "try out" their gifts and "feel out" their ministry desires. Third, new members must develop at least three new meaningful relationships within the first six months of their involvement in the body life of the church.

Notice in the great events at Pentecost that three thousand people were not only converted, but also baptized and added to the church (Acts 2:41). That is what we want to happen in our churches today as well. So if your church is to go from embers to a flame, you will need to cultivate the dynamics of nurture, accountability, encouragement, and friendship within the congregation. In a word, you need to create community in the church. And I know of no better way to do that than through small-group ministry.

The Why of Small-Group Discipleship

I say "small-group discipleship" because I believe that discipleship is best accomplished in small groups. I can get some discipleship done when I am preaching on Sunday, when I am teaching a Sunday school class, and when I am meeting with somebody one-on-one. But the best discipleship takes place in small groups, because that is the primary approach taken by our Lord Jesus when He was planting (and revitalizing) His church. We seldom, if ever, see Jesus discipling people one-on-one in the Gospels, but we often see Him spending time with a small group of men. Even when He was surrounded by a large multitude, He was often speaking specifically to His "small group" of disciples, as in the case of the Sermon on the Mount (see Matt. 5:1–2).

The apostles did not focus on one-on-one ministry either, and I would suggest that this is because we learn best in a group. Learning is not only vertical, but horizontal, in that we need not only a mentor, but also colleagues, or fellow learners. When the truth is taught, it helps to have others besides the teacher affirm the value of those truths. And when error is taught, it helps to have someone question or contradict it, so we will not blindly accept the wrong ideas. When I was in college and seminary, some of my best learning experiences were the regular discussions I had with a group of men at the campus snack shop.

I would also suggest that groups of more than two generally make better use of the discipler's time and effort. There are times when we need to meet with someone individually (one-on-one is for a season and for a reason), but in most cases it makes biblical sense to include more than one. This produces a "geometric expansion" in the discipleship process. For instance, if I want to disciple three men, I could certainly meet with them individually. But if I meet with them together, I accomplish the same thing with all of them at once, and I now have extra time to meet with another group of men. Then, when I've discipled all those men, they will repeat the process with others, and we have geometric expansion.

The How of Small-Group Discipleship

There are many good resources available for small-group ministry, and I suggest that you make use of them in developing your own.[3] But in the following paragraphs I want to outline what I believe are some of the essential aspects of effective small groups.

Interactive Bible study. Teaching in a small group should not be a preaching exercise. Dialogue and discussion should be encouraged, because that approach is more conducive to learning in such a setting. But even though the teaching of the Bible should be done differently from how it is done in the worship services, there should still be teaching. And learning the Word of God should be a primary feature of all small groups, so that we can avoid some of the dangers that they can fall into. An article in *Christianity Today* suggests that many of them "do little to increase the biblical knowledge of their members. Most of them do not assert the value of denominational traditions or pay much attention to the distinctive theological arguments that have identified variants of Christianity."[4] The article goes on to say,

It does not overstate the case to suggest that the small-group movement is currently playing a major role in *adapting* American religion to the main currents of secular culture that have surfaced at the end of the twentieth century. Secularity is misunderstood if it is assumed to be a force that prevents people from being spiritual at all. It is more aptly conceived as an orientation that encourages a safe, domesticated version of the sacred. From a secular perspective, a divine being is one who is there for our own gratification, like a house pet, rather than one who demands obedience from us, is too powerful or mysterious for us to understand, or who challenges us to a life of service. When spirituality has been tamed, it can accommodate the demands of a secular society. People can go about their daily business without having to alter their lives very much because they are interested in spirituality. Secular spirituality can even be put to good use, making people more effective in their careers, better lovers, and more responsible citizens. This is the kind of spirituality being nurtured in many small groups today.[5]

To keep that from happening in your small groups, a central feature in them must always be the accurate teaching of the Word of God.

Intimate fellowship. If it is true that people need to make at least three meaningful relationships in order to be permanently assimilated into a church, then we not only need small groups, but we need small groups that encourage and provide fellowship for those who attend them. The New Testament is filled with commands that we call "the one anothers," and these

181

can help us to plan and evaluate the fellowship in our small groups:

1. Love one another (John 13:34; 15:12, 17; Rom. 12:10; 13:8; 1 Thess. 3:12; 4:9; 2 Thess. 1:3; 1 Peter 1:22; 4:8; 1 John 3:11, 23; 4:7, 11–12; 2 John 5).
2. Live in peace with one another (Mark 9:50; 1 Thess. 5:13).
3. Esteem one another highly (Rom. 12:10, 16; Eph. 5:21; Phil. 2:3; 1 Peter 5:5).
4. Build up one another (Rom. 14:19; 1 Thess. 5:11, 15).
5. Accept one another (Rom. 12:16; 15:5).
6. Admonish one another (Rom. 15:14).
7. Be courteous to one another (1 Cor. 11:33).
8. Care for one another (1 Cor. 12:25).
9. Serve one another (Gal. 5:13; 1 Peter 4:10).
10. Be patient with one another (Eph. 4:2; Col. 3:13).
11. Be kind to another (Eph. 4:32).
12. Be tender-hearted toward one another (Eph. 4:32).
13. Forgive one another (Eph. 4:32; Col. 3:13).
14. Sing with one another (Eph. 5:19; Col. 3:16).
15. Comfort one another (1 Thess. 4:18).
16. Encourage one another (1 Thess. 5:11; Heb. 3:13; 10:24–25).
17. Confess your sins to one another (James 5:16).
18. Pray for one another (James 5:16).
19. Be hospitable to one another (1 Peter 4:9).
20. Greet one another (Rom. 16:16; 1 Cor. 16:20; 2 Cor. 13:12; 1 Peter 5:14).

How could all those commands be obeyed in a church without a small-group ministry? The answer is that they never could, and they never will. So that list makes as good of a case for small groups as can be made, but it also reminds us of what needs to be happening in our small groups.

Intentional ministry. Your small groups will not practice evangelism and other ministries unless you intentionally commit yourself to that. The momentum of small groups will always be toward discipleship and fellowship, which is good. But if you are not careful, it can lead to an introverted, cliquish, and self-centered atmosphere that is not good for anyone there. As one good manual for small groups points out,

> As long as people come to fellowship groups primarily for what they can get out of it, rather than for what they can contribute to it, the groups will be unhealthy and anemic. As long as our deepest commitment is to ourselves, loyalty to the group will be minimal. Jesus came "to seek and save the lost." The activity which energized his life was looking out to needs beyond his own, not an obsession with caring for himself. Therefore, the starting point for mission in our groups is the other members of the group. When we see that life is essentially us and not just me, a deep sense of responsibility and connectedness develops.
>
> This other-centered mindset inevitably translates to the group as a whole looking beyond its immediate needs to the needs of those outside the group.... if a group is to follow Jesus, they will imitate him in mission. Otherwise they will become ingrown, stagnant and lifeless.[6]

Sometimes I have encouraged a small group in our church to invite their unsaved friends for a "Roast the Preacher" night. Then I show up and answer any question they want to ask me. Other groups have planned to invite friends

183

to the Christmas musical, and then planned to get together afterward for dessert. Still others have been involved in regular ministry to homeless shelters and convalescent homes, supporting and encouraging missionaries, etc. What you do does not matter as much as the fact that you are doing something to serve the Lord, and not allowing the group to become stale and self-centered.

Intercessory prayer. There has been a trend in recent years away from Wednesday night prayer meetings and other planned opportunities for God's people to pray. The Bible does not say that we must have meetings just for prayer, but it does very clearly say that we must pray together, regularly and continually. Small groups are an ideal place for that to happen. To put it another way, if your church does not have regular congregational prayer meetings, then you had better be making prayer a major emphasis in your small groups. Otherwise you will be a prayerless church, and you will never go from embers to a flame.

THE DYNAMIC OF DOWNREACH (EQUIPPING)

In the last part of the Great Commission, Jesus says that we should be "teaching them to observe all that I commanded you" (Matt. 28:20). In worship we reach up, in evangelism we reach out, in enfolding we reach in, and we must also be reaching down with sound teaching that flows constantly from the leaders to the members. And remember that the Great Commission itself is one of the commands that Jesus is referring to, so our teaching must have the effect of equipping the members to do the work of the ministry (Eph. 4:11–12).

We have already discussed the importance of teaching and the kind of teaching we should be doing (see chapter 5), so in this section I would like to focus on the fact that Jesus said "teaching them *to observe*..." The goal of our instruction should not merely be to communicate facts, but to produce in our people a faithful, disciplined obedience to the commands of the Lord.

The Necessity for Self-Discipline

It is no mere play on words to say that a church will not be a "discipling" church unless it is first a "disciplined" church. Both terms come from the same root word, of course, and one cannot give away to others what he himself does not have. So the people in your church will not be able to train others in the faith if they themselves have not been trained. But, on the other hand, if their own walk with God is strong, they will be able to use that strength to move mountains for the Lord.

For instance, the church at Jerusalem was a successful discipling church; in fact, it became the first "epicenter" ministry in the New Testament. But notice where that all started. Acts 2:42 says that "they were continually devoting themselves to the apostles' teaching and to fellowship, to the breaking of bread and to prayer." They were devoted, and they were disciplined, committing themselves to certain priorities and intentionally cultivating personal habits of godliness. This might seem to be contradictory to the biblical idea of reliance on the grace of God, but it is not. In fact, any viewpoint on Christian growth that emphasizes "let go and let God" to the exclusion of self-discipline is seriously flawed.

What we need to understand, and teach to our people, is what Jerry Bridges calls "the discipline of grace." In his book by that name, Bridges writes:

Think of yourself seated in a jet passenger plane flying thirty-five thousand feet above the earth. Suppose (I know this can't happen in real life) the pilot were to say through the speaker system, "Folks, we're in real trouble. One of our wings is about to break off." Which one of the wings would you rather lose, the left or the right one? It's a silly question, isn't it? No plane can fly with just one wing. . . . both are absolutely necessary.

Visualize that aircraft as though you were looking down on it from above. . . . You see the fuselage, where you are sitting, the two wings, and the tail assembly. As you look at the two wings you see the words *dependence* on the left wing and *discipline* on the right wing. This airplane illustrates one of the most important principles in the Christian life. Just as the airplane must have both wings to fly, so we must exercise both discipline and dependence in the pursuit of holiness. Just as it is impossible for an airplane to fly with only one wing, so it is impossible for us to successfully pursue holiness with only dependence or discipline. We absolutely must have both.

. . . the point of the airplane illustration is that we must not try to carry out our responsibilities in our own strength and willpower. We must depend upon the Holy Spirit to enable us. At the same time we must not assume that we have no responsibility simply because we are dependent. God enables us to work, but He does not do the work for us.[7]

Let me make the same point in a different way. The Christian life is 100 percent dependence upon grace, and 100 percent disciplined by grace. It is not that we should be 50 percent dependent and 50 percent disciplined, because then we are neither dependent nor disciplined enough. To say that we need to be 100 percent of both may seem illogical, but it is simply supernatural, like the fact that Jesus is 100 percent God and 100 percent man. And just as we should never think that Jesus is any less God or any less man, so we should *always* be depending on God and *always* be disciplined by His grace for His glory.

Titus 2:11–14 says,

> For the grace of God has appeared, bringing salvation to all men, instructing us to deny ungodliness and worldly desires and to live sensibly, righteously and godly in the present age, looking for the blessed hope and the appearing of the glory of our great God and Savior, Christ Jesus; who gave Himself for us, that He might redeem us from every lawless deed and purify for Himself a people for His own possession, zealous for good deeds.

Note that God's grace has brought us three things: salvation (past grace), discipline to deny ungodliness and worldly desires (present grace), and a blessed hope (future grace). When the grace of God brings the work of the Spirit to fruition in our life, we have the "fruit of the Spirit"—love, joy, peace, patience, kindness, goodness, faithfulness, gentleness, and, last but not least, self-control. So we see the Spirit working in and through our own self-discipline.

The Necessity of Church Discipline

If you are going to have a disciplined church, which will then be a discipling church, you will have to teach and practice church discipline. In fact, God will not bless your church with revitalization if you do not commit yourself to obeying Him in this regard. This point is made very clearly by the apos-

tle Paul in his instructions to the church at Corinth. In 1 Corinthians 5, he addresses a situation where a man is openly
involved in sexual sin, and he tells the church to "remove the
wicked man from among yourselves" (v. 13). Then in 2 Corinthians 2:9 he refers to the same situation with these words:
"For to this end also I wrote that I might put you to the test,
whether you are obedient in all things."

It is easy for a church to be obedient in some things, but
it is hard to be obedient in all things—especially the hard work
of church discipline. Yet it is one of the commands of Jesus
that He wants us to teach and observe. In Matthew 18:15–17,
our Lord Himself said:

> And if your brother sins, go and reprove him in private;
> if he listens to you, you have won your brother. But if he
> does not listen to you, take one or two more with you,
> so that by the mouth of two or three witnesses every fact
> may be confirmed. And if he refuses to listen to them,
> tell it to the church; and if he refuses to listen even to the
> church, let him be to you as a Gentile and a tax-gatherer.[8]

When the principles of that passage are taught and practiced in a church, both discipline and discipleship will be happening more and more in our midst. But if they are neglected,
we will experience only the discipline of the Lord (1 Cor.
11:31–32; Rev. 2:14–17).

So, Great Commission discipleship must include the
ministries of exaltation, evangelism, enfolding, and equipping.
Another way of summarizing this inspired plan for church
revitalization is to say that Jesus wants our churches to be
"W.E.L.L." This is an acronym that Greg Laurie uses in his book
The Upside Down Church,[9] and it reminds us that in His last

words Christ called us to worship, to evangelize, to love, and to learn. Christians who do those things are spiritually "well," and spiritually healthy Christians make healthy churches. Healthy churches will be filled with life, and healthy churches will grow for the glory of God.

*Q*UESTIONS

1. Evaluate the worship services in your church, based on the discussion of worship in this chapter. How do you think your worship could be improved?

2. What does it mean that evangelism should be *intentional? A process? Confrontational? Thoughtful and creative? Dialogical? Multifaceted?*

3. Why is small-group ministry so important in a local church? Do you have such a ministry in yours, and how does it compare to the one described in this chapter?

4. Are you merely teaching people in your church, or are you teaching them *to observe,* by promoting self-discipline and practicing church discipline?

5. What are some ways in which you think God will work in your church as a result of your reading and applying the principles in this book? Thank Him for all that He will do, by His grace and for His glory.

What to Do Now

After Peter's sermon in Acts 2, in which he waxed eloquent about the person and work of Christ, the people responded to him with the question, "What shall we do?" (v. 37). Perhaps, after reading this book, you have a similar question in mind. You could use some practical advice about where you should start and how you should proceed, if you want your church to go from embers to a flame. Let me suggest three basic steps, as a good place to begin.

First, you need to make a commitment to the *principle* that the foundational issue is not church growth, but church health and vitality. The local church is a manifestation of the body of Christ. When the body is healthy, it will grow. So what is spiritual vitality? How would it lead to functional effectiveness with the normal anticipation of statistical growth?

It comes through a commitment to the *paradigm* found in Revelation 2:4–5. There Jesus Himself tells the church at Ephesus to remember, to repent, and to recover the first things. He does not tell them to find something new and original to stimulate health and growth, but to return to the time-honored basics that are contained in the Word of God, inspired by God Himself.

Those basic elements of church ministry provide a *process,* to which you and the other leaders of your church must be committed. The process consists of evaluating and addressing each one of the issues we have discussed in this book, which are all "first things" that arise from passages in Scripture that relate to church revitalization. They can be summarized in the "Ten Strategies" that we talk about in our Embers to a Flame conferences and our Fanning the Flame program, in which we shepherd individual churches that are in need of revitalization. All ten strategies are covered in this book, in one way or another, so summarizing them will be a good way to review what you have learned. But they are in a different order here. You can use them as a checklist for evaluating your church and as an outline for your initial discussions with other leaders.

Strategy #1—Connect to the Past.

Connect your church to the vibrancy of its past. Do it with celebration and worship for what God has done, just as the Israelites would pile up stones to teach the next generation what the Lord had done. Celebrate the past victories, investigate and identify the principles that the Lord blessed, and then contemplate how to implement them in the present, remembering that God is the same yesterday, today, and forever. The goal is to have a church that does not live in the past, but does learn from the past, and then lives in the present in order to shape the future.

Strategy #2—Be Gospel Driven and Christ Centered.

The ministry of the Word from the pulpit, teaching classes, small groups, discipleship, and every other ministry must be gospel driven. The church should make a commitment that every time the Scripture is opened, Christ is exalted and explained—who He is as Creator, Redeemer, and Sustainer—declaring the glory of God as revealed in the person and work of Jesus Christ, with special emphasis on the benefits He has purchased for us with His merits. This gospel-driven church would of necessity be Christ centered, since the very essence of the gospel is Christ and Him crucified (1 Cor. 2:2).

Strategy #3—Emphasize Personal and Family Spiritual Formation.

In order to be revitalized, a church must have healthy leaders who then produce healthy Christians and healthy Christian families. A church that has W.E.L.L. leaders will be well led and well fed. Thus, built into the discipleship ministry must be personal and spiritual formation, where men and women are taught the importance of the private and public means of grace, so that the Holy Spirit and the Word of God can enable them to grow in the grace and knowledge of Jesus Christ. Jesus Himself was a model of such spiritual formation, of course. Luke 2:52 says that He grew in wisdom (intellectual disciplines), stature (physical disciplines), favor with God (spiritual disciplines), and favor with man (relational disciplines).

Strategy #4—Prioritize Prayer and the Ministry of the Word.

The vibrant church at Jerusalem was conceived in a prayer meeting and birthed in a sermon (Acts 1–2). A plan for intercessory prayer by the leadership for the congregation should be implemented immediately, as well as a basic strategy for the people to pray for their leaders. And for any church to be alive for Christ, it must have a prioritized ministry of the Word from the pulpit that is faithful to the Scriptures and applicable to the needs of the people in their own generation, with the understanding that the consistent answer is always Christ and the gospel of grace.

Strategy #5—Issue a Call to Repentance.

When the gospel of grace is being preached and taught consistently, the church is prepared to repent of corporate and personal sin. And chances are that a church in need of revitalization is a church in need of repentance. Just as in the days of Achan (Josh. 7), whatever sin is "in the camp" needs to be rooted out with confession and repentance. Perhaps it is the sin of racism, or consumerism, or power struggles, or dealing treacherously with a previous pastor. But whatever it might be, the leadership should lead the church in personal and corporate repentance.

Strategy #6—Be Mission Directed and Vision Motivated.

Your church needs to understand what God has called it to do and what God has called it to be, in the situation where God has placed you. A mission statement and a clearly articulated vision, originating with the pastor and being fine-tuned by other leaders, will lay a foundation on which God's work of revitalization will be built.

Strategy #7—Set Up Small Groups for Discipleship.

The ministry of small groups is not just a good idea, a social invention, or a psychological ploy. It is a biblically derived system that delivers the fullness of discipleship. Discipleship does not take place primarily in the large group as it gathers for worship, though such worship does enhance discipleship. And one-on-one discipleship is helpful for a "season" (period of life) or a "reason" (particular issue of doctrine). But the main delivery system for discipleship is a small group.

Strategy #8—Multiply Servant Leadership.

The work of revitalization cannot begin without one man to whom God has given vision, but it also cannot continue unless there are other godly leaders constantly being raised up to carry out the ministry and carry on the vision. Leadership works, whether it is good or bad, so God will work through good leadership to bring your church from embers to a flame.

Strategy #9—Pursue Missions and World Evangelism.

Missions and world evangelism start in your own backyard, as the church develops an outward focus and a commitment to reaching the different kinds of people within its ministry radius. That local evangelism is then motivated and enhanced by an emphasis on supporting workers and sending them into the harvest in other parts of the world.

Strategy #10—Be Committed to the Great Commission.

All of the strategies for church revitalization find their source, and their greatest expression, in the last words of Jesus to His disciples. And this Great Commission also serves as a thermometer to measure the spiritual temperature of a body, telling us whether it is hot, cold, or lukewarm. A healthy church, according to our Lord, will be committed to UpReach (authentic worship), OutReach (evangelism), InReach (enfolding), and DownReach (equipping).

I am confident that God will bless a church when His work is done in His way. There is hope for the revitalization of any body of believers, even when it has to "rise from the ashes" of decline and failure. Through a commitment to the *principle* of health over growth, the *paradigm* of remember, repent, and recover, and the *process* of the ten biblical strategies, the dying embers of your church can be fanned into a living flame, for the glory of God and the good of His people.

Endnotes

Chapter 1: The Need for Church Revitalization

1. Carl F. George, *Prepare Your Church for the Future* (New York: Fleming H. Revell Company, 1991), 46.

2. Win Arn, *The Pastor's Manual for Effective Ministry* (Monrovia, Calif.: Church Growth, Inc., 1988), 16.

3. Ibid.

4. Lyle E. Schaller, *Create Your Own Future!* (Nashville: Abingdon Press, 1991), 111.

5. C. Kirk Hadaway, *Church Growth Principles* (Nashville: Broadman Press, 1991), 110.

6. Don McNair, *The Birth, Care, and Feeding of the Local Church* (Lookout Mountain, Tenn.: Perspective Press, 1971). See chap. 4, p. 12.

Chapter 2: The Biblical Paradigm for Revitalization

1. Because 1 Timothy was written largely for the purpose of helping a church that was declining, it is an important book for leaders in a church

revitalization project. It should be studied in depth by the entire congregation in a sermon series, or at least by the leaders in their meetings.

2. Matthew Henry, *Matthew Henry's Commentary on the Whole Bible* (Peabody, Mass.: Hendrickson, 1991), 6:906.

3. It seems to me that this makes a good case for a "blended" worship style—not because we should be trying to please everybody in the church, but because we should be trying to represent the nature of God in our worship. Christians and non-Christians alike need to be able to see His character reflected when we worship Him, as Psalm 96 indicates. That psalm is a "Sabbath psalm" that describes God's desire for corporate worship—notice how many times it repeats phrases like "Tell of His glory among the nations" (v. 3) and "Ascribe to the LORD the glory of His name" (v. 8).

4. C. John Miller, *Repentance and 20th Century Man* (Fort Washington, Pa.: Christian Literature Crusade, 1980), 31–32.

5. Ibid., 90.

6. Grand Rapids: Baker, 1991.

7. I once had an opportunity to counsel a depressed pastor whose congregation had dropped from 250 to 150. I discovered, however, that he was ministering in a coal-mining community where many of the people had lost their jobs and moved away during a time of recession. The 150 people who were now in the church actually constituted a much bigger percentage of the local population than the 250 before the downturn. So I encouraged him by pointing out that he was actually reaching more people in his community now—plus he had been there to shepherd those who stayed through a tough time in their lives. So his ministry was successful, despite the smaller numbers.

Chapter 3: The Gospel of God's Grace

1. This corresponds to the classic description of saving faith, in which its elements are described by Latin terms. *Notitia* means that we must know who Christ is and what He has done for us. *Assensus* means that we must be convinced of our own sin and need for Christ. *Volitia* means that we must commit ourselves to the care of the Savior. For more about this, see Louis Berkhof's *Systematic Theology* (Grand Rapids: Eerdmans, 1949), 503–6.

2. For more about this, see John Piper's book *Future Grace* (Sisters, Oreg.: Multnomah, 1995).

3. Bryan Chapell, *Christ-Centered Preaching* (Grand Rapids: Baker, 1994), 12.

4. Another good example of this balance in Scripture can be found in the doctrine of sonship. Our adoption as sons means that God loves us unconditionally—He chose to bring us into His family while we were sinners, and He will always be our loving Father, regardless of how well we perform. But the doctrine of adoption also means that because God is our loving Father, we can expect Him to discipline us in love to make us more like Christ (Heb. 12:5–11). When we are teaching sonship in Christ, it is important to emphasize both truths.

Chapter 4: The Role of Prayer

1. Published critiques of Wilkinson's book include *The Cult of Jabez,* by Steve Hopkins (Burnet, Tex.: Bethel Press, 2002); *"I Just Wanted More Land"—Jabez,* by Gary E. Gilley (Longwood, Fla.: Xulon Press, 2001); and a parody entitled *The Mantra of Jabez,* by Douglas M. Jones (Moscow, Idaho: Canon Press, 2001). In my opinion, each of these critiques has significant weaknesses. Hopkins seems to go to the other extreme at times, advocating an almost ascetic lifestyle. Gilley implies that the prayer of Jabez has very little application to our lives today. And Jones spends more time mocking Wilkinson than shedding light on the issues.

2. Bruce Wilkinson, *The Prayer of Jabez* (Sisters, Oreg.: Multnomah, 2000).

3. Ibid., 76.

4. The Hebrew verb *kavēd,* which is translated "be honorable," can also be translated as "be honored" (as it is in most Old Testament usages). But the consistent teaching of Scripture, which forms the context for this verse, indicates that Jabez was "honored" by God because he was "honorable" before God. For a similar example, see the use of the same form of the word in 1 Samuel 9:6, where Samuel is "held in honor" because he is "a man of God."

5. Toward the end of *The Prayer of Jabez,* Wilkinson quotes a passage that seems to disprove his underlying assumption: "For the eyes of the LORD run to and fro throughout the whole earth, to show Himself strong *on behalf of those whose heart is loyal to Him"* (2 Chron. 16:9 NKJV). Loyalty of heart, not a particular prayer, is the "key to success" in God's eyes.

6. In his parody, *The Mantra of Jabez,* Douglas Jones renders the discovery of Jabez in this way: "I bent over my Bible, and reading the prayer over and over and over, I searched with all my individualistic heart for the future God had for modern people who didn't have decades to cultivate honor" (p. 11).

7. Gilley, *"I Just Wanted More Land"—Jabez,* 18.

8. Gilley writes, "What we have here is the sanctification of selfishness, and of course this is one of the attractions of *The Prayer of Jabez.* . . . Wilkinson's theology is much closer to the prosperity gospel than to biblical Christianity, though he denies it (p. 24). In the prosperity gospel, miracles are constantly being promised when we meet certain conditions. The proof that God will deliver is always based on testimonials, not on the foundation of Scripture. Wilkinson has borrowed a page from the prosperity gospel's handbook and is offering it to Christians, some of whom perhaps have never been exposed to such teaching before. And he is doing so with great success" (ibid., 34–35).

9. Wilkinson tells an anecdote where Mr. Jones goes to heaven and finds a white box, in which "are all the blessings that God wanted to give to him while he was on earth . . . but Mr. Jones had never asked" (*The Prayer of Jabez,* 27). He says, "Through a simple, believing prayer, you can change your future. You can change what happens one minute from now" (p. 29). He says that in heaven God might say, "Let me show you what I wanted for you and tried repeatedly to accomplish through you . . . but you wouldn't let me!" (p. 77). He says that what we do next "will release God's power for you," as if God's power is somehow bound by our choices. All this indicates that he does not acknowledge the absolute sovereignty of God, or at least has not grasped its necessary connection with our prayers. For a good discussion of that connection, see *If God Already Knows, Why Pray?* by Douglas Kelly (Fearn, U.K.: Christian Focus Publications, 1995).

10. The text does not name Jabez's father, but he was probably Ashhur (v. 5). We know from 1 Chronicles 2:24 that Ashhur's father was Hezron, and from 2:9–15 that Hezron was also the father of Ram, who begat Amminadab, who begat Nahshon, who begat Salma, who begat Boaz, who begat Obed, who begat Jesse, who begat David. Jabez was apparently a cousin of Amminadab, so he lived five generations before David—placing him squarely in the time of the judges.

11. Wilkinson, *The Prayer of Jabez*, 20–21.

12. This is because it is recorded in the inspired Scriptures, of course. But it is also interesting to realize that this prayer may have been written before it was offered. Verse 24 says that "they lifted their voices to God with one accord." This could mean that one person prayed, and everyone else prayed along silently in their hearts. But perhaps the prayer was written or memorized, and they recited it together.

13. James Boice, *Acts: An Expositional Commentary* (Grand Rapids: Baker, 1997), 88.

14. I. Howard Marshall, *The Acts of the Apostles* (Grand Rapids: Eerdmans, 1980), 104.

15. John Stott, *The Message of Acts* (Downers Grove, Ill.: InterVarsity Press, 1990), 99.

16. Kelly, *If God Already Knows, Why Pray?* 60–61.

Chapter 5: The Ministry of the Word

1. Robert L. Dabney, *Sacred Rhetoric* (reprint, Edinburgh: Banner of Truth, 1979), 78–79.

2. John MacArthur Jr., introduction to *Rediscovering Expository Preaching,* by John MacArthur Jr. and the Master's Seminary Faculty (Dallas: Word Publishing, 1992), xv.

3. William Hendricks, *Exit Interviews* (Chicago: Moody Press, 1993).

4. G. A. Pritchard, *Willow Creek Seeker Services: Evaluating a New Way of Doing Church* (Grand Rapids: Baker, 1996), 269.

5. John Calvin, *Commentary on 2 Timothy I,* in *The John Calvin Collection* (Ages Software). Calvin also adds these thoughts: "But here an objection arises. Seeing that Paul speaks of the Scriptures, which is the name given to the Old Testament, how does he say that it makes a man thoroughly perfect? for, if it be so, what was afterwards added by the apostles may be thought superfluous. I reply, so far as relates to the substance, nothing has been added; for the writings of the apostles contain nothing else than a simple and natural explanation of the Law and the Prophets, together with a manifestation of the things expressed in them. This eulogium, therefore, is not inappropriately bestowed on the Scriptures by Paul."

6. John R. W. Stott, *The Preacher's Portrait* (Grand Rapids: Eerdmans, 1961), 30–31.

Chapter 6: Leadership Multiplication

1. Stephen Covey, Roger Merrill, and Rebecca Merrill, *First Things First* (New York: Simon and Schuster, 1996), 89.

2. Noel M. Tichy and Eli B. Cohen, *The Leadership Engine* (New York: Harper Business, 1997).

3. Ibid., chapter 7.

4. John Perry, *Unshakable Faith: Booker T. Washington and George Washington Carver* (Sisters, Oreg.: Multnomah, 1999), 313–14.

5. Stanley F. Horn, ed., *The Robert E. Lee Reader* (New York: Grosset and Dunlap, 1949), 468–69.

6. Charles Bracelen Flood, *Lee: The Last Years* (Boston: Houghton Mifflin, 1981), 65–66.

7. Adapted from James I. Robertson Jr., *Stonewall Jackson: The Man, the Soldier, the Legend* (New York: Macmillan, 1997).

8. Horn, *The Robert E. Lee Reader,* 261. The complete letter can be found on page 111 of *The Lee Girls,* by Mary P. Coulling (Winston-Salem, N.C.: John F. Blair Publishing, 1987).

9. Paul Andrew Hutton, ed., *Joshua Lawrence Chamberlain: The Passing of the Armies* (New York: Bantam Books, 1992), 195–200.

Chapter 7: Mission and Vision

1. Another example of a good mission statement is from Faith Presbyterian Church in Sonoma, California, where Dave Swavely, writer of this book, is the pastor: "Faith Presbyterian Church exists for the purpose of bringing glory to God by teaching His Word, worshiping Him in spirit and truth, and loving people in His name, so that many men, women, and children in the Wine Country and throughout the world will be brought into a closer relationship with Jesus Christ by the power of the Holy Spirit."

2. For a discussion of the priority of edification, see pages 149–50.

3. Quoted in *Spurgeon at His Best,* ed. Tom Carter (Grand Rapids: Baker, 1988), 83.

4. Bryan Chapell, *Christ-Centered Preaching* (Grand Rapids: Baker, 1994), 208.

5. See the next chapter for an explanation of "W.E.L.L."

Chapter 8: Great Commission Discipleship

1. Calvin Johansson, *Discipling Music Ministry* (Peabody, Mass.: Hendrickson, 1992), 50.

2. I realize that Jesus knew that the disciples would be scattered around the world as a result of persecution and the destruction of Jerusalem in A.D. 70. But I do not think He was referring *only* to that "going," because the church actually spread the Word throughout Israel and even sent out missionaries to the Gentile nations *before* they were scattered by those events. So Jesus was referring primarily to the "going" of evangelism and missions.

3. Redeemer Presbyterian Church in New York City has extensive and well-written materials available for purchase at their Web site, www.redeemer2.com/rstore/.

4. Robert Wuthnow, "How Small Groups Are Transforming Our Lives," *Christianity Today,* February 7, 1994, 23.

5. Ibid.

6. *Fellowship Group Handbook* (New York: Redeemer Presbyterian Church, 1994), sec. 3.1, p. 1.

7. Jerry Bridges, *The Discipline of Grace* (Colorado Springs: NavPress, 1994), 127–28.

8. For more information about this passage, and biblical church discipline in general, see chapter 8 of *Life in the Father's House,* by Wayne Mack and David Swavely (Phillipsburg, N.J.: P&R Publishing, 1996), or Jay Adams's *Handbook of Church Discipline* (Grand Rapids: Ministry Resources Library, 1986).

9. Carol Stream, Ill.: Tyndale House, 1999.

Index of Scripture

Harry L. Reeder III (M.Div., Westminster Theological Seminary; D.Min., Reformed Theological Seminary, Charlotte campus) is senior pastor of Briarwood Presbyterian Church in Birmingham, Alabama. He previously was pastor of Christ Covenant Church in Charlotte, North Carolina, after serving churches in Chattanooga and Miami. He also speaks daily on the radio program *InPerspective.*

Reeder founded Embers to a Flame, an annual conference on church revitalization. He has written extensively on the subject, led conferences both nationally and internationally for pastors and church leaders, and taught on church revitalization at the seminary level, including Reformed Seminary and Westminster.

An authority on the War between the States, he leads tours of Civil War sites and lectures on such figures as Robert E. Lee, Thomas "Stonewall" Jackson, and Joshua Lawrence Chamberlain.

David Swavely (M.Div., The Master's Seminary) is pastor of Faith Presbyterian Church in Sonoma, California. He has edited a number of books, including *Introduction to Biblical Counseling* by John MacArthur and Wayne Mack. He is author of *Decisions, Decisions,* and coauthor, with Wayne Mack, of *Life in the Father's House.*

For information on Embers to a Flame conferences, including dates and locations, visit www.emberstoaflame.org.